An Enemy DISGUISED

An Enemy DISGUISED

Robert L. Gram

THOMAS NELSON PUBLISHERS
Nashville • Camden • New York

Published in Nashville, Tennessee, by Thomas Nelson, Inc. and
distributed in Canada by Lawson Falle, Ltd., Cambridge, Ontario.

Printed in the United States of America.

Library of Congress Cataloging-in-Publication Data

Gram, Robert L.
    An enemy disguised.

    1. Death—Religious aspects—Christianity.
I. Title.
BT825.G655   1985   236'.1   85-21805
ISBN 0-8407-5942-8

To Torger and Mildred, my parents;
Sarah and Joanna, my children.

C O N T E N T S

ACKNOWLEDGMENTS

Special thanks to the staff, consistory, and congregation of the Fair Street Reformed Church, Kingston, New York; to the editors at Thomas Nelson, especially Larry Weeden for his patience and friendship; and to Gretchen, Bill, and Cathy.

INTRODUCTION

Today we face a crisis in our culture. It is a crisis of faith. Increasingly modern man has trouble believing in the great biblical promise of life after death. For some people, the belief that one's existence continues with God after the respirator is pulled seems like "a tale told by an idiot" or a children's story for the simple-minded. As a minister for twelve years, I have spent a great deal of time with grief-stricken individuals. Many, I find, truly want to believe their loved ones have gone on in the continuing fellowship of God. They want to believe that death is extinguished by renewed life with Christ. But often they cannot. As one widow put it: "Heaven seems as real to me as a three dollar bill." Secular man's inability to believe in the great resurrection promises affects not only how he views another's death; it also colors how he views his own. Without the traditional hope of resurrection, death becomes a terrifying prospect.

This book is about the way people deal with the fear of death when they no longer believe in God's life-renewing power. A little more than twenty years ago, Geoffrey Gorer stated that secular man copes with his fear by sweeping death under the proverbial carpet. In a seminal article, Gorer, an English sociologist, noted the

11

decline of Christian belief among people in western Europe. Church attendance had dropped, and even those who did attend were not exposed, as their parents had been, to the great resurrection proclamation. In order to deal with his fear of death, man ignored it. Or rather he made the subject taboo. Death was no longer considered fit for polite discussion; the word was seemingly stricken from the cultural lexicon. Gorer concluded that modern man dealt with the subject in the same manner the Victorians dealt with sex: he pretended it didn't exist.

Today, however, secular man does not employ the death-as-taboo strategy. In fact, he has moved in the opposite direction. Over the past fifteen years, death has been discussed openly and written about frequently. Often television talk shows feature the latest expert on the subject. Every bookstore, it seems, has at least one shelf devoted to death. There are even clubs whose sole purpose is to disseminate information about dying. In recent history, then, we have moved from a death-repressed to a death-obsessed society. The purpose of this new openness is also to ward off man's fear of death. It is thought the Grim Reaper will lose his sting, so to speak, if we sufficiently dissect, analyze, quantify, and footnote him.

The focus of this book is on particular ideas within the death and dying movement that secular man employs to allay his fear of death. In the vast amount of literature on the subject, certain notions have gained widespread acceptance. Like the hit single that "leaves" the album, these ideas have left their written context and circulate freely in our culture. I believe these notions function as secular religions because they substitute for faith in heaven. C. S. Lewis once noted that the individual may declare that God doesn't exist. Uncomfortable with this vacuum, he quickly fills it with gods of his own making. Similarly, man creates religions, or myths, to allay his fear of death when he no longer believes in the New Testament promise of resurrection. I prefer the word *myths* to *religions* in describing these ideas. The former word, it seems to me, connotes the man-made character of these systems.

The four myths I will discuss are: "The Five Stage Dying Process" (man goes through five sequential stages of dying, the last of which is termed *acceptance*); "The Near Death Experience" (one's life ends with a blissful, out-of-body experience); "Mind over Death" (one need not die if he employs the power of positive thinking); and "Medical Immortality" (death itself will be solved by research). As I have stated, these myths have become secular answers to man's fear of death. They are substitutes of the Christian hope of resurrection.

In order to understand myths on a primary level, we must examine *their common theme* and *their orientation toward death*.

Common Theme

The underlying theme of these myths is that man's knowledge can remove his fear of death. Science rather than theology is perceived by many as the antidote for the Grim Reaper. Emerson once wrote: "Science corrects the old creeds, sweeps away with every new perception our infantile catechisms, and necessitates faith commensurate with the grander orbits, and the universal laws which it discloses." The nineteenth century Transcendentalist expressed an opinion that is more popular today than when he penned the words. In our society many believe that science has superseded religion. Christianity is viewed as primitive thinking that, as such, should be discarded in favor of scientific understanding. In the area of death, it is thought that psychological and medical disciplines have replaced the concept of resurrection, or hope in an afterlife. The myths under consideration are viewed as scientific solutions to man's fear of death.

Orientation Toward Death: Major and Minor Myths

While myths are similar as far as their scientific background, they are dissimilar in their orientation toward death. The assumption behind The Five Stage Dying Process and The Near Death Experience is that man can conquer his fear of death because science has "proved" that dying is a positive experience. The Grim Reaper is really a pussycat, we are told. On the other hand, the assumption behind the myths of Mind over Death and Medical Immortality is that dying is truly an event to be feared. It is, as St. Paul states, man's enemy. Nevertheless it is thought that man's fear can be stilled because science has "proved" that death can be forestalled, or avoided completely.

I consider The Five Stage Dying Process and The Near Death Experience to be major myths because they reflect the prevailing attitude of the death and dying movement. The vast amount of literature on the subject usually describes dying as meaningful, beneficial, or downright blissful. The greatest popularizer of death, Dr. Elisabeth Kubler-Ross, notes that at the end of life the terminally ill patient "emerges from a cocoon with a sense of peace and beauty."[1] That dying can involve emotional or physical hardship is either downplayed or ignored by most popular books written today. On the other hand, the myths of Mind over Death and Medical

Immortality are minor in the sense that they do not reflect the prevailing attitude toward death. Nevertheless, these myths are popular in their own right.

Failure of Myths

Together the major and minor myths constitute alternative belief systems to the Christian hope of resurrection. My concern is that these myths do not free us from the fear of death. Under the crushing weight of illness, they prove to be of little worth. This point was brought home to me by the hospitalization of a friend. A couple of years ago Ted, a self-styled death expert, asked me how I would prefer to die. After noting that I'd prefer not to, I mentioned that a heart attack seemed the easiest exit from life. My answer was greeted with a condescending smile. "I'd rather have cancer," he responded. "Terminal illness allows people to have a meaningful dying experience."

Shocking as it was to me, Ted's statement reflected the faith he placed in the death and dying literature. He particularly bought the myth of The Five Stage Dying Process. Once he described the feelings he thought a terminally ill patient experienced during the final "acceptance" stage; for a moment I thought he was detailing the effects of the latest pleasure drug.

My friend's optimism about dying changed radically, however, when he entered a hospital. Visiting him shortly after his admittance, I found Ted was terrified of an upcoming operation. His surgery was for repair of a minor hernia. If his beliefs couldn't help him face routine surgery, Ted realized, they wouldn't aid him in a medical crisis. Today racquetball has replaced death as Ted's favorite pastime.

I contrast my friend's experience with Esther's. A

member of my church, Esther was a quiet woman of great faith. She entered the hospital for a minor checkup only to be told that cancer had spread throughout her chest cavity, affecting her lungs and heart. The physicians gave her a couple of months to live. Esther was shocked by the diagnosis. She had not experienced pain—just slight discomfort that she attributed to a bout of pleurisy she had had years before. I visited her in the hospital during her final weeks. The Bible was on her nightstand; she read it every evening. "I'm nervous," she told me a week before she died. "I'll miss my sister and brother-in-law. Yet I know I'm going home. There's excitement in that possibility. I have many questions to ask Christ. It will be good to see Mother and Father again." Esther died with a hope the world simply cannot give.

I do not mean to imply, however, that Esther faced mortality like a Stoic. Sometimes in the hospital she was scared. And yet, as she journeyed through dying, her faith increasingly negated the onslaught of fear. Esther never denied the reality of her experience. But she did deny its ultimate significance. Dying for her was not an end, but a beginning, and as such, she could deal with the physical and psychological "birth pains" it entailed.

The same cannot be said for those who adhere to one or more myths. Like Ted, many patients have been victimized by these man-made belief systems. I have known terminally ill individuals who thought that dying would be a positive experience because "science said so." I have known others who believed their cancer could be cured by massive infusions of positive thinking alone, and there were some who thought research had already come up with a miracle cure for their illness. When their belief systems failed, my patients lapsed into despair as well as fear. Instead of solving the problem of death, these myths exacerbated the situation.

The purpose of this book is to expose these secular answers to man's great fear. In the first part of the book, we will explore the cultural soil that made it possible for myths to develop. The second half of the book will describe each myth in detail. By examining false paths, it is my hope that we will see more clearly the one true path that overcomes death's sting.

C H A P T E R

1

An Enemy Disguised

I first became aware of a change in attitude toward death in our society during the late sixties and early seventies. Previously I had assumed that death was something to be feared, an enemy, as Paul put it, which was overcome by Christ's resurrection. But I began to question this assumption with the rise of literature extolling the virtues of terminal illness. In 1970, during my senior year in college, I read Erik Segal's best-selling novel, *Love Story*. The tale concerned the romance between two college students, doomed by discovery of the girl's cancer. Not only did terminal illness increase their love and understanding of each other but, oddly, the disease heightened the young woman's creative capacity. In the hands of the author, cancer became a positive force which enhanced rather than detracted from love. Dying seemed, well, beautiful. A generation wept buckets over the book and subsequent movie.

My initial excursion into the romance of dying occurred six months before I read *Love Story*. In the college library I discovered an article in *Life* magazine about a twenty-two-year-old girl who was dying of cancer. Entitled "A Profound Lesson for the Living," the article described a seminar sponsored by the University of

Chicago's Billings Hospital. At the seminar, terminally ill patients talked about their dying with a helpful psychiatrist. Hidden from the patients behind a screen were a variety of helping professionals. Considered groundbreaking, the program dealt openly with a taboo subject. Not only were physicians, nurses, and ministers able to gain insight about dying from those who were, it was also thought that the exercise was salutary for the patient who had been unable to communicate his needs to others in the past.

What riveted the reader to the page, however, were photographs accompanying the article—photographs of the twenty-two-year-old girl. She was beautiful. Parted in the middle, her hair fell neatly down the front of her blouse as if it had been ironed in place. Her wide-set, almond-shaped eyes were complemented by high cheek bones. The reader was especially attracted to her smile. In one photograph, she tilted her head and laughed at a remark from the interviewer. It was impossible to believe she was dying of acute leukemia.

Like the young woman in *Love Story*, this real-life heroine romanticized dying in my mind. Here was someone who had weeks, perhaps days, to live, and she looked better than most people in the pink of health. Here, too, was someone who, like Ali McGraw in the film version of *Love Story*, seemed to smile in the face of the Grim Reaper. In addition to her photographs, she also romanticized dying by what she said. In the article she joked about her situation. At one point, reflecting on her belief in God, she stated: "When I was little, I always believed in God. I still want to...but I don't know. Sometimes if I talk to somebody, and we talk about not believing in God, I'll sort of look up and think—well, you know—don't believe me. I'm just kidding if you're there."[1] At the close of the interview the psychiatrist thanked the girl for coming. "Oh," she said as if she had a hundred years to live, "anytime."[2]

It was easy for me to read Erik Segal's novel and the article in *Life* magazine and believe that dying had few negative aspects. In fact it seemed that dying was the best experience one could have. Many others received this message from books and articles written at this time. The literature proclaimed the idea that death was beautiful and that dying made people beautiful. If one did nothing but read popular books and attend movies, it would be easy to think that dying was a privilege reserved for the good-looking and youthful.

The romanticizing of death did not begin with *Love Story* or a magazine article. The idea of "good" death has played a role in American cultural history. At the end of the eighteenth and coursing through the nineteenth century, writers made much of the advantages of dying. Terminal illness was the hub around which all sorts of plots revolved. The death of a handsome young man or a beautiful woman was the stock-in-trade story of most American writers. Yet the romanticism of an earlier era differs from the romanticism found today. The reasons why nineteenth century man viewed dying in a positive light are not the same reasons given today. In order to understand the nature of our present love affair with death, we must briefly explore the romanticism of an earlier time.

Death in the Nineteenth Century

In the nineteenth century dying was viewed as a positive experience for two theological reasons. First, dying provided the opportunity to put one's faith in God. In deathbed memoir after deathbed memoir, the hero or heroine overcame physical and emotional problems of dying through belief in Jesus Christ. Focusing on faith vanquished fear and pain.

Second, dying was thought to be positive because it was viewed as the doorway to heaven. In literature today we often read that dying is the "last stage of life." For the nineteenth century romantic, however, dying was primarily understood as the first stage of eternal life. Thus in much of the popular literature of that era dying was positive because it was the testing ground of faith and the gateway to heaven.

The account of Martha Neal is typical of the deathbed genre. Written in 1817 by her mother, the account is ostensibly historical. Throughout the nineteenth century, however, the distinction between fiction and nonfiction is blurred. The typical dramatic devices found in short stories and novels are also at work in historical accounts. The young woman's final days are described in the following words:

> Mr. Brown, our worthy pastor, asked her if she did not wish to return again to the world, and enjoy its pleasures? Her answer was, that she desired to be resigned to the will of God; that every dispensation of his providence might be sanctified to her; but if Jesus would receive her, she would rather depart; she would give up all for blessed immortality; and should she be restored to health, her only wish was to live to the glory of God.

> She desired to become a member of the "Female Praying Society;" and she requested an interest in the prayers of all that called upon the name of Jesus. In this state of mind she continued three weeks; when it was thought advisable to give a slight mercurial affection to the sys-

tem, which it was hoped would entirely relieve her. She then devoted herself entirely to religious inquiry; she became more than ever engaged for herself at the throne of grace; and though racked with pain of body, and her mouth extremely sore, she employed her whole time in reading, singing, and praying. Thus she continued growing ripe for the glory; when three days before her death, it pleased the Lord to dispel her doubts and fears, and give her a sweet assurance of pardoning mercy through a crucified Redeemer. Her emancipated soul was absorpt in Divine love—her tongue was set at liberty to utter the praises of him who "by the blood of the Covenant delivered her out of the pit where in there is no water." She exclaimed in raptures of holy joy, "Dear mother, I have found Jesus! He is precious to my soul! Have you ever seen Jesus? He is all in all, he will save poor vile Martha. I thought I loved you, dear mother, but I find I love my precious saviour better—Oh! how precious he is to my soul! The one altogether lovely. Now, my dear mother, you said you would give me up if he would manifest himself to me as he does not to the world: weep not then for me; but pray for resignation." She then drew her affectionate arms around me, and prayed a considerable time. After a few moments she sang the hymn "Happy Soul, Thy Warfare's Ended;" and with a countenance beaming with holy joy exclaimed, "Come Lord Jesus and receive vile Martha to thyself before the light of another morning." With these words she became insensible; her body was permitted to suffer two days longer: then, without a struggle, she departed to join the song of the ransomed, "Worthy is the Lamb that was slain to receive power, and riches, and wisdom, and strength, and honour, and glory, and blessing."[3]

As we can see from this stylized, sentimental account, terminal illness became a testing ground for faith. We are privy to Martha Neal's final struggle. There is no attempt by her mother to downplay her daughter's pain. Generally if there is a distortion of reality in deathbed stories, it is on the side of pain. The agony of terminal illness may be exaggerated to highlight the victory of faith. In the account before us, suffering is meaningful because it brings the young girl closer to Christ. Suffering is also meaningful because we are aware that faith can overcome the greatest human catastrophe.

The second component in most deathbed memoirs, the belief in resurrection, is also stressed in our account. Perhaps the most common literary device in fiction and nonfiction at this time is the lengthening of the final moments of life. Deathbed scenes are never short. They go on for days, sometimes weeks. The expansion of time allows the hero or heroine to quote long-forgotten verses from the Bible or a Sunday school primer, sing hymns, or deliver sermons all pointing to the glory of the resurrection. In our present account, Martha Neal not only witnesses to those by her bed, she is seemingly transported to that other realm by rapturous joy. As the century progressed, the dying heroine became more concerned with detailing the specifics of heaven. Often she spoke about the lifestyles, occupations, eating habits, and methods of childcare in the kingdom. No detail was overlooked.

The nineteenth century reader perceived dying as a positive experience because of its association with Christianity. This is not to say that he thought death was intrinsically good; it was viewed as the Grim Reaper. Nevertheless, from a theological perspective, dying was positive inasmuch as it was overcome by the power of faith and hope of immortality.

Let me make it clear that nineteenth century literature

on death is not a model of Christian orthodoxy. In its graphic depiction of the dying process and in the artificiality of the patient's "farewell address," the deathbed memoir has far more in common with second century accounts of Christian martyrs or fourteenth century narratives by Christian mystics than it has with the writings of St. Paul and the Gospels. Indeed there are many touches in the deathbed memoir that would make the biblical writers cringe. In the latter half of the nineteenth century, for example, some episodes contained seance scenes in which the terminally ill patient acted as a medium for departed spirits. Many memoirs also extended the deathbed scene to the cemetery. Thus conversation between parents and their departed son or daughter continued at the grave. In spite of such flourishes, deathbed memoirs do reflect the biblical tie between death and faith.

The New Romanticism

Unlike the literature of the nineteenth century, no such tie with Christianity exists in the writings of the new romantic wave. Dying is good in *Love Story* and the *Life* magazine article not because of its link with faith; indeed, strong religious commitment is conspicuously absent in the accounts written during the late sixties and early seventies. If one studies the literature of the period he sees that dying was positive because of its link with science. This is especially evident in nonfiction accounts like "A Profound Lesson for the Living." This article was one of the first to hint that science had solved, in a manner of speaking, the problem of death.

The article in *Life* was not primarily about the beautiful, leukemic girl, but rather about the psychiatrist who interviewed her—Dr. Elisabeth Kubler-Ross. "A Profound Lesson for the Living" served as advance publicity for a book by the Swiss psychiatrist. Entitled *On Death and Dying*, it proved to be the single most influential piece of writing in the burgeoning death and dying field. In the article, as in the book, Kubler-Ross hinted that psychiatry had discovered a solution to fear of dying.

The problem, as the psychiatrist viewed it, was not dying itself, but social attitudes toward the subject. People feared what they didn't understand, and their fear was transferred to the terminally ill patient. Thus the sick individual was trapped by a death-denying society. He could not express his needs to those he loved because they were too afraid to broach the subject with him. Surrounded by "a conspiracy of silence," the patient was afraid of death because he was forced to die alone, unaided by emotional support from others. The message of the article and the book was that dying is not intrinsically frightening.

By removing the negative connotations from dying itself and placing them on society, Kubler-Ross offered a solution to death. If the helping professional could free the individual from the cultural conspiracy of silence by offering him the opportunity to share his feelings, the patient's fear would vanish. "Talk therapy" would be the liberating factor. The beautiful young woman in *Life* became photographic proof that talk therapy, in the hands of a psychiatrist, worked.

The new romanticism was far different from the romanticism of the nineteenth century. Martha Neal overcame her fear of dying through faith in Jesus Christ. The anonymous young woman in *Life* magazine overcame her fear by faith in science, particularly behavioral science. Beginning in the late sixties and early seventies, therapy superseded theology as an answer to the fear of death. If one could talk out his fears, it was thought, they would cease. Thus science, or a branch of science, rather than Christianity, became the vehicle in which death was viewed in a new light.

The Rise of the Death and Dying Movement

Why did the *new romanticism of death* in the late sixties and early seventies begin? Why did dying become a chic topic at this time? In order to understand the reasons, we must turn once again to Elisabeth Kubler-Ross, for it is her book that launched the current surge of interest in the subject. *On Death and Dying* became the bible of the movement and catapulted its author into the national spotlight.

In rereading her book, I discovered that it contained two interrelated ideas that appealed to society at the time. First, Kubler-Ross attacked medical technology. This is ironic; for although Kubler-Ross offered a scientific answer to the fear of dying, she nevertheless rejected aspects of medical science. People were afraid to die, wrote the psychiatrist, because death became associated with large, impersonal hospitals. The patient viewed dying as an isolated, depersonalized event because, throughout his hospital stay, he lived in an isolated, depersonalized environment. Machines aided the conspiracy of silence. They served as barriers we erected to shield ourselves from the terminally ill and death itself. Kubler-Ross wrote:

> [The patient] may cry for rest, peace, and dignity, but he will get infusions, transfusions, and a heart machine, or tracheotomy if necessary. He may want one single person to stop for one single minute so that he can ask one

single question—but he will get a dozen people around the clock, all busily preoccupied with his heart rate, pulse, electrocardiogram or pulmonary functions, his secretions or excretions but not with him as a human being....Is the reason for this increasingly mechanical depersonalized approach our own defensiveness? Is this approach our own way to cope with and repress the anxieties that a terminally or critically ill patient evokes in us? Is our concentration on equipment, blood pressure our desperate attempt to deny the impending death which is so frightening and discomforting to us that we displace all our knowledge onto machines, since they are less close to us than the suffering face of another human being which would remind us once more of our lack of omnipotence, our own limits and failures, and last but not least perhaps our own mortality?[4]

The corollary to this idea is that people accepted dying in the good old days before technology shielded them from communication. There was a halcyon era, Kubler-Ross implies, in which dying was as natural as apple pie. In her book, the psychiatrist described an early childhood episode in which a farmer was fatally injured in a fall. The farmer spent his last days at home, under the watchful eyes of family and friends. Allowed to die in a familiar environment, his end proved to be as uplifting as his life. According to Kubler-Ross, dying was a natural event before the advent of x-rays, heart machines, and other death-denying accouterments of society.

That dying is fearful because of medical technology and that dying was a positive experience in a pretechnological age are two ideas that are highly debatable. Nevertheless they were readily accepted by the youth-oriented culture of the late sixties and early seventies.

In 1969, the same year *On Death and Dying* was published, the largest segment of American society came of age. Angry with their country, those born after the Second World War protested American foreign and domestic policies. On college campuses students burned flags and draft cards to protest our involvement in Vietnam. Environmentalists blocked the entrances to plants that polluted air and water. Civil-rights demonstrators pitched their tents and listened to speeches near the Washington monument. Our television screens were filled with scenes of confrontation. On the nightly news we grew accustomed to the sound of bullhorns and sight of exploding tear-gas cannisters.

Youth's disenchantment went far beyond a nation's specific policies. The postwar generation often viewed modern society as innately evil. Technology, in all of its forms, became the enemy. Industrialization stripped the worker of his identity and worth, young people believed, and automation replaced human initiative with the unthinking efficiency of machines. Although the individual could protest issues like the war in Vietnam, how could he possibly demonstrate against progress itself? The task seemed overwhelming. In their frustration, radical groups like the Weathermen vented their anger at technology by randomly destroying property of corporations. Many more young people retreated into a pretechnological world of their own making. Communes sprang up in rural parts of the country. Young people migrated from the city to life on the farm, replete with woodstove, compost heap, and organically grown food. Books that stressed the joys of rustic living became best sellers.

The youth movement protested technology and lauded a pretechnological world. Kubler-Ross's theory on dying contained both ideas. While youth attacked the "military industrial complex," the psychiatrist attacked the medical industrial complex. While youth took to the hills in reaction to modernity, the crusader hinted that death, like life, was far better in a pretechnological society. Kubler-Ross's message found a ready home among young people. Having gone to college and seminary during the late sixties and early seventies, I can vouch for the hold she had on my generation.

I remember attending a lecture she gave at a leading university in the East shortly after her book was published. The gymnasium was packed with students and faculty, philosophical groupies who had come to hear our newest leader. We applauded as she spoke about the plight of terminally ill patients in our large, technologically advanced hospitals. We listened intently as she talked about her native Switzerland and friends who died peacefully at home, unencumbered by intravenous tubes and monitors. She captured our hearts. She was one of us.

Because Kubler-Ross appealed to the cultural mindset of the time, we bought her understanding of death lock, stock, and barrel. Technology rather than death itself became the enemy. We believed that the medical industrial complex had contaminated the dying experience the way corporations had polluted air and water. The answer was to view death apart from the social and technological environment. If we could, we would find, like the rustics of another era, that death held no terror.

A new romanticism of death had emerged. Unlike the romanticism of the nineteenth century, the Gospel of the Good Death took as its source science, in the form of messianic psychiatry. This gospel would quickly permeate society.

2

Modern Society's View of Death

Kubler-Ross's *magnum opus* created great interest in a once taboo subject. Appearing at the right moment, *On Death and Dying* appealed to the American mindset of the late sixties and early seventies. Overnight, it seemed, dying had become a problem of science rather than theology. Christianity contends that fear of death is part of man's makeup. But after 1969, at least in the popular mind, man's fear was viewed as a cultural phenomenon which, like other social ills, could be ameliorated by scientific understanding.

The purpose of this chapter is to examine briefly the development of popular scientific literature on the subject of death and dying. What were the important themes that were passed down and modified by Kubler-Ross's successors? "Happy-Death" literature and books that stress the victory of science over the Grim Reaper will be examined. In each case, I'll deal with the impact books have made on specific institutions. To what extent has the death and dying movement affected our culture? Have we moved from a death-repressed to a death-obsessed society?

In order to understand the death and dying movement, we must examine the phenomenal growth of literature on the subject. When I write of the *movement*, I am discussing books that share certain themes—many books. Robert Fulton, one of the foremost authorities on the death and dying movement, states that hundreds have been written since 1969. According to Fulton, popular literature on the subject is increasing exponentially.

Today one can find literature on the subject in any library or bookstore. The books appeal to a variety of tastes. To borrow the spiel of a used-car dealer, "There's a paperback just right for you." Children's books like Patricia Giff's *The Gift of the Pirate Queen* explain to the young reader how natural death is. There are books for adults which detail the joys of dying (e.g., Richard Boerstler's *Letting Go: A Holistic and Meditative Approach to Living and Dying*). The plots of fictional accounts like *Love Story* and novels based on true incidents like *Heartsounds* are centered around the beautiful dying experience. Then there is nonfiction like Barry and Suzi Kaufman's *A Land Beyond Tears*, which seemingly employs fictional devices to heighten the drama.

Death and dying literature is geared to people with various degrees of education—and books that make little sense to any group. On my desk is a paperback entitled, *The Lazy Man's Guide to Death and Dying.* On the cover is a fellow who looks like the leather-jacketed chief of a motorcycle gang. A blond, overweight angel escorts him out of the world. The book is not satiric, religious, or, for that matter, coherent. The author rambles about cosmic consciousness and pleasant sensations that accompany dying. According to Roberta Halporn, owner of the largest mail order bookstore devoted exclusively to death, *The Lazy Man's Guide* sells well.

Development of the Happy Death Literature

Two major themes developed from Kubler-Ross's work. The first was the "conspiracy of silence," a seminal idea that recurs in death and dying literature of the early seventies. Essentially it meant that Americans verbally hide what they fear. According to Kubler-Ross and her imitators, the conspiracy of silence robs the terminally ill patient of the support he needs. When the individual tries to discuss his dying, friends and relatives quickly divert conversation to the weather. More important, the mavens of death and dying believed that the "conspiracy" is the cause of man's fear of death. Because of cultural reticence, a natural process is invested with sinister connotations. Dying as a somber experience is an idea foisted upon the terminally ill patient by a death-denying society.

There is partial truth to the notion of a "conspiracy of silence," as anyone who spends time in a hospital knows. Ministers often become primary listeners for the terminally ill, when families, who are paralyzed by fear, refuse to broach the subject. It is not uncommon to see a patient verbally struggle with relatives who have unintentionally turned a deaf ear. Although open communication is an important part of therapy, it is not the panacea to man's fear of death. Even those who can express themselves openly to loved ones often approach the end of life with teeth chattering dread. Reading the death and dying literature, however, gives one the impression that lifting the conspiracy of silence is all one needs to conquer fear.

The "conspiracy" idea proved useful by providing an easy solution to a difficult problem. Indeed the solution became so easy that a bit of magic slips into this literature. As the death and dying movement developed, it was thought that merely saying the word *death*—like the incantation of a witch doctor—could lift the conspiracy of silence. The therapeutic approach of Earl Grollman is typical. A popular writer in the death and dying field, Grollman tries to defuse children's fear in the following manner:

> When you die, you're dead. Try saying that word DEAD. It is a hard word to say, isn't it? Not hard to pronounce, really, but hard to make yourself say. Maybe because it's a sad word...even a little frightening. Let's say it again: DEAD. Now let's say another word: DIE. That's what happened to grandfather. Grandfather died. He is dead.[1]

Besides providing an easy solution to the problem of death, simply saying the word enhanced the dramatic possibility of death narratives. In the last chapter, we saw an example of nineteenth century deathbed literature. The account of Martha Neal was ostensibly historical, and yet it contained certain stylized elements common to the deathbed genre. In the same manner, saying the word, *death* serves, I believe, as the fictional chink in the nonfictional edifice.

Barry and Suzi Kaufman's best seller, *A Land Beyond Tears*, is typical. The story concerns Maggie Millen, and how her husband and two children try to ignore the fact she is dying of cancer. The disease is never mentioned, and communication in the household never moves beyond small talk. It is Kaufman, a social worker, who helps the family break the conspiracy of silence. In a sentimental scene, he gets Sammy, the seventeen-year-old son, to acknowledge his mother's impending death:

"I'm...I, it," he stuttered, squeezing out the words with extreme difficulty. "When I...lift the, the pan, I know! I know! I know!" He began to shout. His fingers dug into his face. "I know. Nobody will tell me, but I know! She's...she's...she's going to...die." Sam screamed the last word. He stood up, snapping his body off the wood plank, and gaped at me—surprised, confused, relieved. For a long time he held his breath, his body remained rigid, frozen at attention like a young soldier. A sudden gust of wind ripped through his hair, moving his curls like grain in a farmer's field. Suddenly, he groaned and dropped down on the bench.

I moved closer to him. "Sammy, I'm here. I'm still with you. How do you feel?"

"Weak. Like I have a fever." He stared down at the track and said, "Die. Die. Oh, God, I was so scared to say it. And now look. Die. Die." He smiled queerly. "It's not so bad. Why did I think it would be so bad?"[2]

Sammy's admission is the turning point of the story. Having mastered his fear of death by speaking the taboo word, he is able to help his sister and father. The conspiracy of silence is lifted and, by the last chapter, everyone is talking openly to Maggie about her illness. Stories in which saying the proscribed word solves the death dilemma abounded in the midseventies.

It was but a short step from the idea that death was easily managed to the notion that dying itself was pleasurable. Kubler-Ross never stated as much in her book *On Death and Dying*. She did note, however, that terminally ill patients reach a stage of acceptance before they die, "an existence," as she put it, "without fear or despair."[3] The Swiss psychiatrist also noted that the last stage of life is similar to infancy: "And so, maybe at the end of our days, when we have worked and given, enjoyed ourselves and suffered, we are going back to the stage that we started out with and the circle of life is closed."[4] Although dying is viewed as a neutral event, nevertheless a degree of romanticism slips into Kubler-Ross's language. The prophet of thanatology opened the door to more positive interpretations of dying by noting that one's end is like one's beginning.

In his book, *Overcoming the Fear of Death*, David Cole Gordon noted that death, "the ultimate unification experience,"[5] is similar in effect to orgasm. Gordon's book appeared a year after the publication of *On Death and Dying*, and yet his outlook is far more positive than Kubler-Ross's tome, to say the least. Gordon, however, was ahead of his time. It was not until 1975 that the idea of blissful death really took off.

In 1975 Raymond Moody, a medical student with a Ph.D. in philosophy, authored a book entitled *Life After Life*. The slim volume became a best seller and, apart from Kubler-Ross's initial work, the most important volume of the death and dying movement. Moody charted the experiences of 150 men and women who had come close to dying. According to the author, people whose vital signs had ceased for a brief period described the same sensation when they regained consciousness. They said they felt as if they were moving out of their bodies toward a mysterious being of light and a higher plane of reality. Moody hinted that his findings verified religious and philosophical speculation about a future life. Science might one day confirm what prophets and sages knew all along.

Life After Life did more than present a rosy, non-denominational picture of immortality. It also left the reader with the impression that the passage from one life to the next was beneficial and, yes, pleasurable. The "interim state," the patients noted, sharpened their human capacity. They could relax and remember more than they could in their healthy state. The patients also noted that the near death experience, as Moody called it, was euphoric, beyond description. Their accounts are similar to descriptions of drug trips by LSD users.

After Moody's book author after author jumped on the literary bandwagon. The joys of dying were sketched in greater detail. Dying became more beneficial than the latest self-help book, and more pleasurable than the effect of the latest narcotic. Even the Queen of Death herself, Elisabeth Kubler-Ross, viewed the subject from an increasingly optimistic perspective. In 1978 she could write that the terminally ill patient is like a butterfly who "emerges from a cocoon with a sense of peace and beauty."[6] Dying, she believed, helped individuals "become creative beyond any expectations."[7] Like the death and dying movement in general, Kubler-Ross's thinking evolved in a cheery direction. During the midseventies, then, death and dying literature shifted in emphasis from breaking the conspiracy of silence to enumerating the joys of dying itself. In less than a decade, death moved from a neutral entity to a positive force.

Is there truth in the idea of blissful death? I have seen people in the hospital die without pain. Some were aided by narcotics; others were not. A recent study indicates that 50 per cent of those with terminal cancer experience little distress prior to death.[8] Being free from pain, however, is a far cry from the state described by many popular writers in the death and dying field. Certainly the idea of a blissful ending is absent from the pages of medical journals.

Impact of the Happy-Death Literature

The glut of books detailing the joys of dying affected society in a number of ways. First, let me deal with its impact on educational institutions. Happy-death literature can be found in university, seminary, and medical school libraries. From what I have seen, there is little attempt to cull the wheat from the chaff. Professor Vanderlyn Pine, professor of sociology at the State University of New York at New Paltz, and one of the leading authorities in the field, views the happy-death literature as a mixed blessing. He realizes such books have stimulated interest among students. Nevertheless, because of authors like Kubler-Ross and Raymond Moody, Dr. Pine's charges come to class with a good deal of misinformation which impedes scholarly pursuit.

In 1973 seventy colleges offered courses on death and dying. Altogether there were about six hundred courses on the subject in America. In 1981 Kubler-Ross noted that over a hundred thousand courses were offered on nearly every college campus. While many instructors are well trained, many more are not. According to Dr. Pine, substantial numbers of teachers have been nourished on a diet of happy-death books. Thus misinformation, especially on the junior college level, abounds.

Happy-death literature has made an impact on seminaries and medical schools, although administrators are loath to admit it. In the midseventies many theological and health institutions employed the hands-on method of death education that Kubler-Ross pioneered at the Billings Hospital in Chicago. Terminally ill patients were brought in by the bus load to speak to ministers, physicians, and nurses.

Having attended more than thirty-five such seminars, I am convinced they serve as evidence for the prevailing belief in both theological and medical schools that, once the conspiracy of silence had been lifted, dying would be viewed as a neutral, if not positive event. Faculty and students alike romanticized the drama played before them. It seemed these budding thanatologists clung to every word of the terminally ill patient, as if they were privy to the speech of a god. Even banal statements were mined for hidden meaning. The attitude at these gatherings was reverential as well as sympathetic. The terminally ill patient, however humble his mental capacity, was viewed as a guru of the first order. It was thought that dying conferred enlightenment that the healthy could not attain.

Today the death and dying seminar is no longer in vogue. Nevertheless there is still a degree of romanticism about the subject in hospitals and seminaries, if we believe the articles by health and theological professionals criticizing the romantic assumptions of their alma maters.

Happy-death literature has affected more than institutions of higher learning. It has trickled down to secondary schools as well. In 1973, *Time* magazine reported that a significant number of high schools were offering courses on the subject to meet student demand. The photograph accompanying the article showed a ninth or tenth grader trying a coffin on for size. Visiting funeral parlors and morgues were requirements for many courses. One teacher, who had become the resident thanatologist at his high school, noted that "death is not morbid but exciting, dynamic."[9] Since 1973, the curricula for secondary students has increased. A recent survey indicates that one in four high schools offers programs on death education. Having examined the curricula of several schools in my area, I find that students are taught that dying is a natural event if it is approached openly.

Although there are few statistics here, it seems that the happy-death thinking has percolated down to the primary levels as well. Articles have been written to help teachers make death palatable for children. Several weeks ago a friend told me how his son's nursery school teacher used the death of the child's much-loved dog to initiate discussion about the joys of mortality. The boy was not assured by his teacher's optimism. Children are realists. The boy understood correctly that the death of his best friend was an unnatural occurrence that abruptly sundered an important relationship. According to my friend, his son had no idea why his teacher tried to whitewash the reality of death.

Death Clubs

The happy-death literature has affected more than schools. It has also given rise to institutions, "death clubs" if you will, of its own. In the midseventies groups formed that were devoted to principles of certain books. The idea of the good death became the organizing idea for new secular cults. These groups are still active today.

In Los Angeles, the "Threshhold Research Center" offers the services of a "death and dying companion" who, for a fee, will come to your home and discuss the positive aspects of your imminent demise. The group EXIT pays housecalls to help plan your suicide. Then there is the organization in Florida that tried to preach the gospel of the happy death to inmates on death row. In California "Life Force" has developed a therapy designed for cancer patients. The basic assumption behind "cancering" is that a trained specialist can help the patient reach a point of "childlike transparency," to use the phrase of one of the group's leaders, Dr. Richard Turner. For forty-five dollars an hour, Turner can help the individual discover "an air of lightness" in the death experience. You need not be terminally ill to benefit from death clubs. Groups like "The Dying Project" and "The Dying Center" urge people to make the most out of dying by contemplating its rewards while they're still healthy.

By far the most important and widespread death club is Kubler-Ross's "Shanti Nilaya," an expression that means "home of rest" in Sanskrit. Having written several best sellers, the Queen of Death decided to go a step further and franchise death and dying centers in 1977. Shanti Nilaya represents the McDonalding of death. Today there is at least one center in every state of the union. Like all of the happy-death clubs, Shanti Nilaya's primary purpose is to enrich the lives of the healthy rather than meet the needs of the dying. At a center one can enroll in a host of courses that will help him deal with the rest of his life. The individual can take courses in "Rebuilding and Refocusing" ("Participants will gain insights into how the mind uses emotions to perpetuate itself"); "Intensive Caring Seminars"; "Training in the Externalization Process" (Grades 1 and 2); "Weekend Training Workshops" ("Ten guests are invited who would like to participate for the purpose of working through their own personal issues"); and "Drawing Interpretation" classes.[10]

Central to Shanti Nilaya is the five day "Life, Death, and Transition" workshops which Kubler-Ross conducts at Shanti Nilaya centers throughout the country. The "L.D. & T.", as it is called by knowledgeable folk, consists of seventy people, including terminally ill patients and parents of dying children. According to Kubler-Ross, "The emphasis of the workshop is on YOU, to help you get in touch with any negative aspect of your being (fear, shame, guilt, hostility, etc.) thus enabling you to work better with dying patients and/or other people."[11] In a recent Shanti Nilaya newsletter, several graduates summed up what the L.D. & T. workshop had taught them:

> Keep it simple. Let the universe handle the details.
> Should you shield canyons from the windstorms, you would never see the beauty of their carvings.
> Everyone is your teacher—especially those who push your negative buttons. Bless them.
> You don't necessarily get what you want, but what you need.[12]

After reading the course descriptions and the quotes from the L.D. & T. graduates, one comes away from Shanti Nilaya with the belief that dying has become the organizing principle for pleasure itself. Generally death and dying clubs are similar to the human potential groups that sprouted like kudzu in the late sixties. The only difference is that groups like Shanti Nilaya have substituted a romantic view of dying for hallucinogenic drugs or Far Eastern mantras.

Science-over-Death Literature

Let me turn to the glut of books that can be lumped under the rubric of "science over death." Kubler-Ross's *magnum opus* also stimulated the production of books that placed a premium on mankind's ability to overcome the Grim Reaper. The emphasis is not on the dying experience itself, but rather on the scientist's ability to alter the course of mortality. Two streams of thought developed simultaneously among the authors of "science over death."

First, the idea of man-made immortality became a popular issue in 1969 with the publication of Alan Harrington's book *The Immortalist: An Approach to Engineering Man's Divinity.* Harrington noted that science would solve the problem of death sooner than most people believed. According to the author, only minor obstacles were left on the road to immortality. Using the language of a crusader, Harrington urged the scientific community to complete the task: "Death is an imposition on the human race," he wrote, "and no longer acceptable...mobilize the scientists, spend the money, and hunt death down like an outlaw."[13] Man's sole religion, noted Harrington, was the scientific quest for immortality. He wrote:

> Our faith must accept as gospel that salvation belongs to medical engineering and nothing else; that man's fate depends first on the proper management of his technical proficiency; that we can engineer freedom from death not pray for it; that our messiahs will be wearing white coats, not in asylums but in chemical and biological laboratories.[14]

Although Harrington's book achieved a cult following, it was not until the midseventies that like-minded prophets reached wide audiences. Perhaps the individual who did most in the field was Albert Rosenfeld, whose book *Prolongevity* became a best seller in 1976. Rosenfeld gave a clear-cut timetable for the approach of "immortality engineering." Through enzyme, hormone, and DNA research, mortality would be conquered by

43

2025, although initial success would occur in the mid-eighties. Date-setting on the dust jacket was the commercial come-on people needed to buy Rosenfeld's book. Other authors followed suit. Indeed, in order to spark interest, writers kept shortening the time before the big breakthrough. Alvin Silverstein's best seller, *The Conquest of Death,* is typical. The following sentence appeared on the dust jacket of his book, published in 1979: "If you survive the next ten years, you may live on indefinitely in youth and vigor—you may become immortal."[15] Such literary gimmicks attracted readers to the cause.

Here, too, we must question the basic assumption. Although science has increased man's life expectancy, it has not come close to abolishing death as popular pundits predict.

The second stream of science-over-death books stresses the power of the mind over disease. It is thought by writers of this genre that a positive mental attitude can forestall death. The first book to trigger popular reaction was Lawrence LeShan's *You Can Fight for Your Life: Emotional Factors in the Causation of Cancer.* In the midseventies LeShan, a psychoanalyst, administered personality profile inventories to cancer patients and conducted psychotherapy on a number of terminal cases. From his research he concluded that one's personality contributed to cancer. The individual who could not accept the loss of a central relationship or express resentment was a likely candidate for the tumor clinic. LeShan suggested that one could avoid disease by changing one's responses to life crises. An infusion of optimism was worth more than simply an ounce of prevention. Optimism also functioned as the pound of cure necessary to defeat a cancer in progress. *You Can Fight for Your Life* is sprinkled liberally with stories of tumors shrunk by the power of positive thinking.

A year later LeShan's book was superseded by Norman Cousins's work, *Anatomy of an Illness.* Cousins told how he overcame a life-threatening cartilage disease by large doses of vitamin C and a steady diet of Marx Brothers films. Although he makes mention of the importance of modern medicine, the theme of his book is literally "Laughter is the best medicine." On the power of the mind, Cousins wrote:

> No medication they [physicians] could give their patients was as potent as the state of mind that a patient brings to his or her own illness. In this sense...the most valuable service a physician can provide to a patient is helping him to maximize his own recuperative and healing potentialities.[16]

Certainly since Hans Selye's classic work on stress,[17] modern man has been aware that the mind influences the body in diverse ways. That certain diseases can be caused or exacerbated by negativity is beyond question. One gains the impression from books like LeShan's and Cousins's, however, that a healthy mind is all one needs to be disease free. That the power of positive thinking is the cure-all or even the most important component of healing is a far cry from what responsible medical technicians tell us.

Impact of the Science-over-Death Literature

Like happy-death literature, books that stress science over death are found readily in college, medical school, and theological libraries. Like Kubler-Ross, Rosenfeld and Cousins have made their impact on educational institutions. Although their books are less well known than *On Death and Dying,* their theories have been debated in as many academic journals as writings of the happy-death movement. Cousins's book, for example, has been written up in top medical journals like *Lancet* and the *Journal of American Medicine.* Science-over-death literature has not found its way into secondary and primary grades the way happy-death literature has, but it has made a definite impact on society.

Death Clubs

The works of Harrington and Rosenfeld, among others, have legitimized death clubs that were previously in existence. In 1967 James Bedford, a seventy-three-year-old psychology professor, died of cancer. Moments after death, chemicals were pumped into his corpse and he was packed in dry ice. Several hours later his body was stored in a deep freeze "thermos" of liquid nitrogen. James Bedford was the first individual to be cryogenically interred. Since 1967 about two dozen corpses have undergone the same procedure. The disciples of cryonics believe the frozen dead will be resurrected when man's knowledge unlocks the secret to immortality.

Bedford's burial made headlines and national attention was drawn to the small California-based group with which he had been affiliated. Cryonics soon became a synonym for contemporary lunacy. By the late sixties the movement had been derided in print and on television. Indeed, it seemed every stand-up comedian had a joke on the subject. According to Dr. Constance Lindhorst, an expert in this area, public perception of cryonics improved with the release of books like Rosenfeld's which stressed the imminence of immortality. The number of cryonics groups is still small. Yet, as Dr. Lindhorst notes, individuals in the movement are no longer regarded as crackpots. Beginning with Harrington's *The Immortalist*, the raft of science-over-death books has brought cryonics into mainstream American thinking. The movement is viewed as a legitimate, albeit expensive, way to deal with the problem of death.

Books like Rosenfeld's have also stimulated the growth of groups that believe cryonic interment soon will be obsolete. Noting the imminence of a scientific breakthrough, clubs like "Omega Fitness" state that immortality is a possibility for members—if they take care of themselves. Physical fitness is elevated to religious dogma. In an introductory booklet to Omega Fitness (an organization with chapters in Arizona, Idaho, and Oregon), one reads that the member's task is "to keep himself at an optimum level of physical health until the 'Great Day' arrives." According to the booklet, science will establish, "a second Garden of Eden, where death will be an unheard of word." All this will come about by the year 2000. Until that time Omega Fitness offers advice on what to eat, drink, and wear ("Loose fitting clothes allow blood to circulate freely through the human system"), as well as "Exercises for an Immortal You."[18]

Hospice

I believe the science-over-death literature has also affected the American hospice movement. In 1967 Dr. Cicely Saunders opened the first modern hospice in London. Her primary concern was to relieve the pain of the terminally ill. Because of St. Christopher's, the world first heard of the Brompton's Cocktail, so named for the physician who first used it. Composed of heroin in an alcohol and cherry-syrup base, it is one of the strongest euphoriants ever invented. Today the "cocktail" has been replaced by a variety of painkilling medications that are geared to make the last weeks of a patient's life as comfortable as possible.

At St. Christopher's the emotional needs of the patient are also met. Guests are welcome anytime and, unlike many health-care facilities, children are encouraged to visit loved ones. Personal habits like smoking and drinking are allowed. The individual may even bring furniture and a pet. Although everything is done to ensure the psychological well-being of the patient, the primary responsibility at St. Christopher's is the relief of chronic pain.

Dr. Saunders's model was imported to America when the National Cancer Institute gave an eight hundred thousand dollar grant to Hospice, Inc. In 1974 the first hospice was established in New Haven, Connecticut. Today there is at least one in every state. Although the American movement, like its English counterpart, stresses the primacy of drug therapy for the relief of pain, this principle is modified in some hospices. Often nonmedical personnel buy the notion that it is the power of the mind as much as, if not more than, the effect of the hypodermic that relieves physical distress. In other words, there is a strain of thinking in the American hospice movement that downplays the role of narcotics in pain relief.

Addressing this issue, Hastings Center researchers David Smith and Judith Granbois warned: "If a physician who is an expert in symptom control is not in charge, the patient suffers, for symptom control is not something laymen can accomplish."[19] Many laymen, however, think they can. In fact they are often encouraged by staff who have little medical background. At our local hospice, for example, a Dr. Gabriel Cousens was asked to lecture volunteers about his views on holistic healing. I quote the secretary's summary of Dr. Cousens's talk:

> He presented meditation as a way of working with questions of the meaning of life, death, and life beyond death. He said that human beings have four basic kinds of pain: physical, social, role (job, role in life), spiritual. Meditation enables one to "let go" of the effects of these various kinds of pain and to find the quiet space within ourselves from which we gain perspective on the cosmic and holistic realities of which human beings are a part. "What we understand as love is really our own inner love shining outward and being reflected back to us by the mirrors of those we love. Death—either our own or our loved one's—shatters that mirror. An alternative at those times is to use meditation to help us to connect with the quiet source of love, the SELF, to sustain the dying and those around them."[20]

Dr. Cousens's teaching is a psychological narcotic, a Brompton's Cocktail of the mind that minimizes the terminally ill patient's possible need for medication. According to Dr. Cousens one can simply meditate physical distress away. Hospice volunteers were taught that they had a part, perhaps a bigger part than they imagined, in managing pain control.

Ideas like those expressed by Dr. Cousens are found in other centers for the dying, especially those not directly affiliated with a hospital or medical center. Recently I conducted an informal survey of hospices in my area. In sixteen out of nineteen, mind-over-disease books like

Anatomy of an Illness were either recommended or required reading for hospice volunteers. In thirteen hospices I found Stephen Levine's *Who Dies* and Deborah Duda's *A Guide to Dying at Home* on bookshelves. Like Cousens, both authors believe that physical distress can be controlled by the mind. In fact they indicate that pain is positive, because it forces the individual to view himself as more than a body. Levine even offers meditations to help the terminally ill to use their pain for the expansion of consciousness. In one exercise, Levine advises:

> Don't try to capture the pain. Let it float free. No longer in the grasp of resistance. Softening. Opening all around the sensation...Let the pain soften. Let the pain be. Let go of the resistance that tries to smother the experience. Allow each sensation to come fully into consciousness. No holding. No pushing away. The pain beginning to float free in the body.[21]

Science-over-death literature has found its way into the American hospice movement. Will the hospice volunteer, as dedicated as he is, talk to the patient about a "softening process" when he should be calling for the physician?

This ends our brief survey on the development of the death and dying literature and its impact on society. Let me note that the literature has been transformed into movies and television dramas. Radio talk shows also provide fertile ground for the spread of faddish notions about death. Generally our society believes that science, as it is found in popular literature, has thrown light on the subject of our darkest fears. Although there is some truth in what Kubler-Ross and Norman Cousins tell us, why do we accept their ideas completely, uncritically?

Larger questions loom. Why do we believe science answers questions that Christianity cannot? Why have we elevated the technician in the white coat while denigrating the preacher in the black robe? We will grapple with these questions in the next chapter.

C H A P T E R

3

The Formation of Modern Myths

We live in an age when science forms our view of reality. Because the myths under consideration are perceived as scientific answers to the problem of dying, we must briefly explore the reason we place faith in man's achievements. At one time the United States could justly be called a Christian culture. Even if the individual was not religious in a formal sense, generally he accepted the idea that a Supreme Being had a hand in running the affairs of state. John Jay, Chief Justice of the Supreme Court, expressed the prevailing colonial sentiment when he wrote: "God governs the world, and we have only to do our duty, and leave the issue to him." Less than a hundred years after Jay wrote those words, science had begun to replace God as the governing principle in society. The purpose of this chapter is to sketch the way science appropriated the position in culture once held by Christianity. Our study will focus specifically on the impact of scientific theory on Christians. As we shall see, believers as well as nonbelievers were affected by the spirit of the scientific age.

The Rise of Science

In the late 1700s theology and science were closely connected. The Bible was viewed as a scientific work, giving accurate statements about geological forms, the creation of plants and animals, and the early history of man. It was thought the emerging sciences would corroborate the truths in Genesis. To the Enlightenment thinkers in Europe and America, science would serve theology. The eighteenth century Dutch mathematician, W.J.S. Gravesande, expressed the prevailing opinion when he wrote: "That the world was created by God is a Position wherein Reason so perfectly agrees with Scripture that the least Examination of Nature will show the footsteps of Supreme Reason."[1]

On both sides of the Atlantic, it was thought that the Bible was the textbook of natural history as well as God's ultimate word of salvation. Thus the faithful were tested at the beginning of the nineteenth century when the emerging sciences, geology and paleontology particularly, challenged the biblical account of creation. The findings in rock strata indicated a world much older than the six thousand year period of traditional exegesis. Scientists also discovered vast changes in plant and animal life over the millennia. In the eighteenth century it was thought that life forms described in Genesis had undergone no change. Then fossil hunters uncovered extinct flora and fauna that are not mentioned in the Bible. This new information called the first two chapters of Genesis into question or suggested that the Bible did not tell the complete story.

The findings of geology and paleontology were reconciled to the biblical account by the development of cataclysmic theology. On his accession to a professorship at

Oxford in 1819, William Buckland noted that his teaching would attempt "to shew that the study of geology has a tendency to confirm the evidences of natural religion; and that the facts developed by it are consistent with the accounts of creation and deluge recorded in the Mosaic writings."[2] The key to Buckland's thinking was the Flood. The world before Noah set sail was much different from the one he found upon leaving the ark. Because of God's mighty act, the flora and fauna had changed drastically. To explain modifications at different rock strata, the Catastrophists, as they were called, theorized that God had caused a series of floods that were not recorded in the Bible. For a brief period Buckland and his followers patched the rift between science and theology.

Before Christians could sit back in their chairs and relax, however, a new challenge appeared. In 1830 Charles Lyell, an English geologist, published the first volume of *Principles of Geology,* in which he refuted the claims of cataclysmic theology. Lyell argued that changes had come about through ordinary geological means—erosion, volcanism, earthquakes—acting gradually over a long period of time. The past could be understood by observing geological processes in the present. Lyell noted that extinction occurred when geologic changes affected climatic conditions; thus successive transformations of plant and animal life could be understood apart from "God's mighty acts." Although Lyell's theory (popularly dubbed *Uniformitarianism*) accounted for changes in plant and animal life, it did not explain the origins of species. God was still the creator, a position that Lyell himself maintained until the latter years of his life.

The real crisis between science and theology came in 1859 with the publication of *The Origin of Species* by

Charles Darwin. Why is there a relationship among species instead of a random distribution of forms? the British scientist asked. Why, for example, are the bones of the arm of a man, the foreleg of a dog, and the wing of a bird built on the same general plan? And why do similar organisms behave in similar ways? Why, for example, do men and orangutans express sadness by weeping? Why do men and horses yawn? For Darwin, all questions could be answered if species were related by a common ancestor. According to the British naturalist, evolution is the change that species undergo in order to adapt to their environment.

In 1871 Darwin published *The Descent of Man and Selection in Relation to Sex* in which he worked out his theory with regard to man. Tracing our ancestry, Darwin wrote:

The Simiadae then branched off into two great stems, the New World monkeys; and from the latter, at a remote period, Man, the wonder and glory of the Universe proceeded.

Thus we have given to man a pedigree of prodigious length, but not, it may be said, of noble quality. The world, it has often been remarked, appears as if it had long been preparing for the advent of man: and this, in one sense, is strictly true, for he owes his birth to a long line of progenitors. If any single link in this chain had never existed, man would not have been exactly what he now is. Unless we willfully close our eyes, we may, with our present knowledge, approximately recognize our parentage; nor need we feel ashamed of it. The most humble organism is something much higher than the inorganic dust under our feet; and no one with an unbiased mind can study any living creature, however humble, without being struck with enthusiasm at its marvelous structure and properties.[3]

At first Christians were aghast at the consequences of Darwin's work. The idea that man and apes shared an ancestor dislodged the idea that *Homo sapiens* were made in the image of God. A second consequence was just as critical for theology. It was thought that the best evidence for God's existence was the highly specialized nature of organisms. The complex design of the human hand or the woodpecker's beak required by logic the presence of a Grand Designer. Darwin stated, however, that such sophistication was the product of adaptation to environment. Thus, a Grand Designer was no longer needed to explain the intricacy of life forms.

Darwin's theories fractured the mindset of the nineteenth century. Matthew Arnold, a poet and essayist, aptly described his age as "an iron time of doubts, disputes, distractions, fears." The son of a clergyman and a student of science, Arnold described midcentury man as "a wanderer between two worlds, one dead, the other powerless to be born."[4] In a remarkably short period of time, however, Darwinism permeated Western consciousness the way an infant's cry fills the delivery room. By the 1870s most American scientists believed in evolutionary theory. Prophets like historian John Fiske and publicist Edward Youmans spread the new gospel to the masses.

Perhaps the most popular spokesman was Robert Ingersoll, know to the nation as "The Notorious Infidel." Ingersoll represents the common intellectual attitude toward religion in the post-Darwinian age. Reacting against his father, a Calvinist clergyman, he spent his life ridiculing "barbarities" he found in the Old and New Testaments. He addressed thousands, attacking dogmatic and illiberal elements in Christendom. Ingersoll offered a new faith. Science, he noted, was "the only true religion, the only Savior of the world."[5]

The Christian Response

Darwin's research became the straw that broke the Christian's back. Before *The Descent of Man* theologians held the line against scientific skepticism. After this seminal work religionists lost faith in their own arguments. Indeed, after seven decades of intellectual war, it seemed the scientist could refute any defense of traditional faith the theologian offered. Christians abandoned the struggle, either by rejecting science outright or by adapting themselves to the new philosophical environment. Since the majority of believers practiced accommodation, we will focus on this historical trajectory.

Christian leaders were initially shocked by evolution, but soon they fell in with the spirit of the age and tried to incorporate Darwinism into Christianity. I use the word "tried" for many, like James McCosh, realized the difficulty of the task. President of Princeton University and one of the foremost representatives of Presbyterianism, McCosh accepted much of Darwin's thinking, yet balked at its implications. We sense his unease in a section of his book *Christianity and Positivisim*. McCosh wrote:

> I am inclined to think that the theory contains a large body of important truths which we see illustrated in every document of organic nature; but that it does not contain the whole truth, and that it overlooks more than it perceives.... That this principle is exhibited in nature

and working to the advancement of plants and animals from age to age, I have no doubt....But it has not been proven that there is no other principle at work.[6]

In McCosh's scheme a Grand Designer fashioned man's special attributes. God and Darwin could coexist, however tenuous the relationship. Many clergy over-looked the problems McCosh sensed. Creating a theology purified by science seemed more important than defending the sovereignty of God. Shailer Matthews, Dean of the Divinity School at the University of Chicago, insisted that "the starting point for religion, as for any other form of behavior, is a relationship with the universe described by the scientist."[7] Matthews believed that long-held doctrines like the Virgin Birth should be jettisoned if they failed to meet empiric standards. Calling himself a Modernist, Matthews described the new believer as one who "starts with the assumption that scientists know more about nature and man than did the theologians who drew up the Creeds and Confessions."[8]

Parish ministers along with the theologically elite joined the evolutionary bandwagon. The *Independent*, the most widely read paper among clergy, reflected the positive light with which Darwinism was viewed by its constituents. Noted clergymen Henry Ward Beecher and Lyman Abbott were outspoken supporters of the new science. The interest ministers took in Darwin can be gleaned from an interesting letter Edward Youmans wrote to Herbert Spencer, a leading spokesman of evolution in England. In this snippet Youmans appropriates revivalist phrases in recounting a clerical group's "conversion."

The clergy are in a flutter. McCosh told them not to worry, as whatever might be discovered he would find

design in it and put God behind it. Twenty-five clergymen of Brooklyn sent for me to meet them on a Saturday night and tell them what they should do *to be saved.*
I told them they would find *the way of life* in the Biology
and in Descent of Man. They said "very good," and
asked me to come again at the next meeting of the clerical club, to which I went and was again handsomely res-
oluted.[9]

Of this period, Columbia historian Richard Hofstadter wrote:

Religion had been forced to share its traditional authority with science, and American thought had been
greatly secularized. Evolution had made its way into
churches themselves, and there remained not a single
figure of outstanding proportions in Protestant theology
who still ventured to dispute it.[10]

Although the clergy reconciled Darwinism to Christianity, parishioners had great trouble. Perhaps they saw
more clearly than their leaders that science had eroded
the foundation upon which their faith was built. Americans had been taught to believe that the Bible was a
book of science as well as religion. For many, faith was
predicated on the literal truthfulness of God's "textbook"
in regard to the flora and fauna of the world. Thus when
seventy years of scientific skepticism reached its apogee
under Darwin, people's faith crumbled. If the Bible was
inaccurate about aspects of creation, including man's
descent, what other mistakes would Darwin's successors
discover? Was Jesus himself a fabrication? During the
last two decades of the nineteenth century, many people
left churches and embraced science as the new religion.
Many more adopted a dualistic attitude toward Christianity. The Bible might not explicate the working of the

natural world, but it was accurate in its description of spiritual reality.

In order to accommodate Darwin, Christians developed dualistic thinking to salvage their faith at the end of the 1800s. Reflecting the popular mindset, Lymann Abbott wrote: "In so far as the theologian and evolutionist differ in their interpretation of history...I agree with the evolutionist, not with the theologian."[11] Increasingly the natural world was viewed as the domain of science alone. Man was master on earth; God was sovereign in heaven. In 1888 John Parsons, a professor of chemistry at Harvard, could write about two orders of truth, science and Christianity. Although he believed faith occupied the higher realm, he felt the two orders never met.[12] Christians maintained their position by separating the religious and scientific spheres, and then reducing the importance of the latter.

The deathbed literature reflects the growing dualism in religious thinking at this time. In 1853 Henry Harbaugh, a popular Christian writer, noted: "The piety of the time has too little heaven in it....It seeks too much to woo heaven, and yields too little to being wooed by it."[13] In less than a decade Harbaugh's statement no longer applied to the American scene. Books that stressed the specifics of afterlife began to dominate popular literature.

The most famous writer of the "heaven-our-home" era was Elizabeth Stuart Phelps, whose books *The Gates Ajar* (1868), *Beyond the Gates* (1883), and *The Gates Between* (1887) were models of consolation literature. Phelps's purpose was to paint the glory of heaven in earthly pastels. Historian Helen Sootin Smith notes that God's kingdom, in Phelps's hands, became "an utopian analogue of the world she knew, complete with hospitals for sick souls who receive the ministrations of spirit doctors until they can assume full citizenship in the city of God."[14] In *The Gates Ajar,* the most famous volume of the trilogy, Aunt Winifred describes the kind of mountains and trees one will find in heaven:

> Yes; mountains as we see them at sunset and sunrise, or when the maples are on fire and there are clouds enough to make great purple shadows chase each other into lakes of light, over the tops and down the sides,—the ideal of mountains which we catch in rare glimpses, as we catch the ideal of everything. Trees as they look when the wind comes through them on a June afternoon; elms or lindens or pines as cool as frost, and yellow sunshine trickling through on moss. Trees in a forest so thick that it shuts out the world, and you walk like one in a sanctuary.[15]

Aunt Winifred goes on to describe idealized flowers, homes, and musical instruments in heaven. In her two sequels, Phelps devoted greater attention to the particulars of the kingdom. We learn, for example, the methods of courtship and the eating habits of the angels. She even describes a speech that Beethoven delivers to a rapt celestial audience.

The dualistic mentality that developed in the last decades of the nineteenth century is also reflected in gravestone design and epitaphs. Of this era in funeral art, historian James Curl writes:

> With the discoveries of Charles Darwin...faith was rocked to its foundations, and the Victorians were racked by doubts and searchings. At the same time, many accepted the literalness of the Victorian heaven, peopled as it was with angels, cherubs, and other wonderful creatures.[16]

When we examine cemetery sculpture in England and
the United States, we see the literal nature of the Victorian heaven carved in marble. Besides angels and cheru-
bim, tombs were decorated with doves, lambs, deer, and
harps—symbols of an idealized, bucolic afterlife the deceased and his relatives hoped to find. That heaven
would be like home is seen also in accouterments like
chairs, beds, sofas, books, and houses that adorn burial
plots during this period.

Epitaphs describe earth as a "suburb of the life elysian" and heaven as "the home of the blest," sentiments
that were lacking in earlier inscriptions. During the first
six decades of the nineteenth century, epigraphy focused
primarily on the state of the deceased ("Christ called at
midnight as I lay, in thirty hours was turned to clay") or
on the resurrection itself ("The boiling coffee on me did
fall,/And by it I was slain,/But Christ has bought my
liberty,/And in Him I'll rise again").[17] By the 1880s,
however, the emphasis had shifted to statements describing the hills and streams, the homes and mansions
awaiting the pilgrim.

The developing dualism is also reflected in the school
primers and hymns of the era. In McGuffey's *Fourth Eclectic Reader,* to cite one example, many of the poems focus on the heavenly home still to come, a change over
earlier editions. The closing lines of one poem is a fair
representative of the group:

> How beautiful will brother be
> When God shall give him wings
> Above this dying world to flee
> And live in heavenly things![18]

The same theme can be found in the glut of hymns

which mark this revivalistic era. William Hunter's paean to heaven is typical of the hymns sung in churches and at tent meetings:

> My heavenly home is bright and fair
> No pain no death can enter there
> Its glittering towers the sun outshine
> That heavenly mansion shall be mine.
>
> Let others seek a home below
> Which flames devour or waves overflow
> Be Mine the happier lot to own
> A heavenly mansion near the throne.[19]

To summarize: At the beginning of the nineteenth century science was perceived as the handmaid to theology; by the end of the century, science had threatened to supplant it. Living in a post-Darwinian era, the average Christian faced a crisis of faith. He felt abandoned by the leading thinkers of the day, religious as well as secular, who seemingly had left biblical literalism for evolution. To maintain his faith, the Christian separated heaven from earth, then put greater emphasis on the former, the realm of God. He made heaven real by depicting it in supraearthly terms. Thus earth, the realm of science, became little more than an imperfect model of a far greater but familiar reality.

Shift from the Heavenly to the Earthly Sphere

Christians were able to maintain their faith as long as they believed in the reality of heaven; it became increasingly difficult to do so, however, as the new century dawned. The reality of heaven gave way to a materialist understanding of cosmos. In other words, earth, the realm of science, seemed to be the only truth for modern

man, Christian or otherwise. What created this percep-
tual change? Although there were several factors, let me
isolate one that stands out in my mind. I believe the rise
of corporate America, with its need to find markets for
goods, created a consumption-oriented culture that sold
the idea that ultimate reality resided in objects. During
the first three decades of the present century, there was
an effort on the part of the captains of industry to rede-
fine consciousness in a way that was amenable to the
goals of manufacturers.

In 1919 Edward Filene, who was known as the mouth-
piece of industrial America, noted that "mass production demands the education of the masses; the masses
must learn to behave like human beings in a mass production world....They must achieve not mere literacy
but culture."[20] *Culture* for Filene and other magnates was
synonymous with consumption. When he made his remark, industrialism had reached a stage at which it
could provide the basic material needs of a culture.
Thus, in order to sustain themselves—to keep selling
new products—companies created pseudo-needs which
could be satisfied by the acquisition of an ever-increas-
ing variety of products. The key to their success was advertising.

In 1928 Edward Bernays, a nephew of Sigmund Freud
and a pioneer in public relations, wrote: "If we understand the mechanism and motives of the group mind, it
is now possible to control and regiment the masses according to our will without their knowing it."[21]

According to Bernays and other social psychologists,
the way to influence people was to refashion their understanding of personality. Character was no longer an in-
herent quality, but rather something one acquired from
the outside world. Industrial spokesman Floyd Henry

Allport noted that "our consciousness of ourselves is largely a reflection of the consciousness which others have of us.... My idea of myself is rather my own idea of my neighbor's view of me."[22]

Admen diffused the idea that one's personality was shaped and defined by external elements like family and friends. By inculcating a sense of self-scrutiny in the average American, Madison Avenue psychologists were able to maneuver him all over the product chessboard. In order to protect oneself against social ostracism, one acquired the right product. In order to measure up to society's standards, one bought the proper dress, the right car. A Cutex Hand Preparation advertisement found in a 1920 issue of the *Ladies Home Journal* is typical of the psychological strategy of the time:

> You will be amazed to find how many times in one day people glance at your nails. At each glance a judgment is made.... Indeed some people make a practice of basing their estimate of a new acquaintance largely upon this one detail.[23]

Increasingly the individual defined his self-worth, his personality in terms of the products he purchased. By pitting the individual against society, advertising reduced modern man to a "commodity self," to use the phrase of historian Stuart Ewen. Everything positive about the individual could be attributed to his judicious selection of products. Subtly Americans were led to believe that the material world was the only reality. Materialism became the American creed. Thus science, which dealt with the earthly, the material, gained ascendency. With the rise of Darwinism, God's sovereignty had been confined to heaven. With the emergence of industrialization in the first three decades of the twentieth century,

God and heaven seemed little more than the dream of a child. The churchgoer might pray and recite creeds; nevertheless he was haunted by the thought that an invisible world was a nonexistent one.

Our Scientific Culture

Up to this point I have confined my writing to the impact of natural sciences on the Christian. Let me add briefly that theories of natural science, particularly evolution, shaped political and behavioral hypotheses that, in turn, affected the person in the pew. In other words, the findings of natural science colored major thought streams of the nineteenth century. The writings of Karl Marx languished until his followers claimed his theories were scientific formulations. At Marx's funeral in 1883 Friedrich Engels, the coauthor of *A Communist Manifesto*, eulogized: "Just as Darwin discovered the law of organic evolution in human history, so Marx discovered the law of economic evolution in human history."[24] In passing Marx off as a scientist, Engels won a new audience for their movement, and Marxism spread quickly beyond the borders of England and Germany.

Borrowing from Darwin, Sigmund Freud viewed himself as a psychic evolutionist whose principle of infantile sexuality explained the nature of man's development as accurately as the theory of natural selection. "Science," Freud wrote, "is no illusion. But it would be an illusion to suppose that we could get anywhere else what it cannot give us."[25] By noting that his theories were scientific, Freud gave his worldview legitimacy.

In the writings of both Marx and Freud, the theological mindset had to go. Certainly Christians had inferred as much from the works of Lyell and Darwin, yet these major thinkers in the field of natural science had no personal ax to grind against religion. Near the end of his life, Darwin could write: "I have never been an atheist in the sense of denying the existence of God; I cannot remember that I ever published a word directly against religion or the clergy."[26] Marx and Freud, on the other hand, hated religion, and deliberately sought to discredit it. In reading the literature of both, the reader is presented with an either-or proposition. Either it is their theories or it is religion. One can't have both. Noting Marx's aversion to Christianity, Georg Jung, a peer of the young philosopher and his radical friends wrote:

> If Marx, Bruno Bauer and Feuerbach come together to ground a theological-philosophical review, God would do well to surround Himself with all His angels and indulge in self-pity, for these three will certainly drive him out of His heaven....For Marx, at any rate, the Christian religion is one of the most immoral there is.[27]

Freud, too, had profound contempt for theism. In his book *The Future of Illusion*, he dismisses religion as "wish fulfillments" and God as nothing more than an imaginary father substitute. In another work he wrote of religion: "The whole thing is so patently infantile, so foreign to reality, that to anyone with a friendly attitude to humanity it is painful to think that the great majority of mortals will never be able to rise above this view of life."[28]

Freud underestimated people, for as the twentieth century dawned, the great majority began to "rise above" the Christian worldview. Not only had the findings of natural science pushed Christians into a corner, but political and behavioral thinkers, appropriating scientific jargon, used their theories to undermine the reality of Christian faith. The hope of heaven was assaulted by scientific materialism, a common phrase that defines Marxism as well as the psychic materialism of Freud, in which the mind holds the key to reality. Bombarded by science in a variety of directions, man lurched into the twentieth century, an era whose characteristic mark, according to the *Chronicle of Higher Education*, "is a loss of faith in transcendence."[29]

We are steeped in science. Jacques Barzun has described our society as one in which

> the ideas and products of science have filtered—unevenly, incompletely, with results good and bad, but so marked that they affect the whole unmistakably. The test is simple: not only does such a society support and respect many varieties of scientific workers, but these are so placed that their work gives off emanations, practical and spiritual, which affect every part of culture.[30]

We are aware of science not only in technological areas like nuclear energy and state-of-the-art household appliances; we are also cognizant of the social sciences and the experts in these fields who flood the media with their findings. Sitting on a prime-time television show, the scientist quantifies human experience, especially in the areas of sex, depression, and self-esteem, shelling the audience with, what one wag calls, "pseudo-mathematical decoration."[31] Even the minutia of daily existence comes under the scientist's scrutiny. Recently a radio newscast informed me that a professor in California had discovered that executives who put on their shoes, beginning with the left foot, are generally more content than those who start with their right. Common to the newscasting industry, such information indicates the extent science has permeated mundane aspects of human existence.

No one escapes the "emanations," to quote Barzun, of science. Even fundamentalist Christians, whose spiritual forebears turned their backs on Darwin, are affected by the spirit of the age. My point is illustrated by the controversy in recent history over "creation science" in the public school curricula. In 1981 more than fourteen states introduced legislation requiring that creationist views of life's origin (a "prime mover" creating life out of nothing) be taught along with the theory of evolution. The most publicized case involved the state of Arkansas, whose legislature passed a pro-creationist bill in March 1981. The constitutionality of the law was challenged in a U. S. District Court two months later. The plaintiffs contended that "creation science" is a veiled attempt to import God into the public schools, thus violating the First Amendment. Fundamentalists argued that the law "advances both scientific inquiry and academic freedom. Scientific inquiry is advanced by providing students with an alternative scientific theory to evolution science."[32]

In order to prove its point, the defense brought more scientists to the witness stand than the plaintiffs. One comes away from the controversy with the opinion that fundamentalists value the authority of science as much as their opponents. While rejecting the spirit of the age in one sense, creationists support it by carrying out their battle within the scientific realm. In Arkansas, and other states, it was as if both sides agreed that science represented the highest order of truth.

Science affects all of us. Because of its ubiquitous nature, it is easy to have faith in it. We are bombarded by ideas that all presume to be scientific, and we no longer have the strength or will to question whether they are. In other words, science is taken as truth in our society, even if we cannot verify the scientific claim. Dress a television actor in a physician's smock, for example, and he can sell anything from medicated throat lozenges to the Brooklyn Bridge. His pitch is irresistible if he intones, "Four out of five doctors recommend...." Cultural historian Christopher Lasch notes that in our society "truth has given way to credibility, facts to statements that sound authoritative without conveying authoritative information."[33] Anything that *sounds* scientific, we believe, *is* scientific.

Besides its ubiquitous nature, we place faith in science because, like religion, we perceive it as a mysterious entity. Throughout much of the nineteenth century, it was thought that science could be understood and mastered by the common man. This attitude had its roots in post-Reformation Europe, and continued to exert influence until the rise of Darwin. Increasing knowledge brought specialization, and soon the sciences were removed from the realm of the everyday. According to Isaac Asimov, modern man finds that science "is complex and chilling. The mathematical language of science is understood by very few."[34]

Man places faith in mysterious aspects of life, whether he is a primitive watching lightning, or a modern viewing the results of nuclear fission. We place faith, too, in the "keepers of the mysteries" as well. Philosopher Theodore Roszak writes: "People may still nostalgically honor prescientific faiths but no one—no priest or prophet—any longer speaks with authority to us about the nature of things except the scientists."[35] That we have faith in the practitioners of the mystical arts is seen, for example, in the power we give to physicians. Until quite recently, the idea of getting a second opinion about one's illness seemed unthinkable. We still believe all physicians are equally capable, equally infallible.

We place faith in myths of dying because they are part and parcel of the scientific milieu that dominates our thinking today. Ironically, as we shall see, myths are rejected as unscientific by factions of the scientific community. Half-truths at best, the components of these thought systems are as unverifiable as religious dogma. By attacking the scientific credibility of myths, I hope to undermine faith in them. Perhaps, too, in a larger context, by playing science against itself, I will dent the faith we place in the monolithic structure, science, itself. Even if myths represented the best science had to offer, they would still be unable to save man from what he fears most. Faith in Jesus Christ can accomplish what man's knowledge never can.

C H A P T E R

4

The Myth of the
Five Stage Dying Process

Kubler-Ross's myth is, by far, the most popular with which we shall deal. One authority notes that "the widespread acceptance of her now famous five stage theory is without precedent"[1] Rare is the helping professional who cannot name the levels through which the terminally ill patient purportedly progresses. The medical laity may not be able to do so; yet most believe dying is an evolutionary process that leads to a peaceful, if not blissful, end. The Five Stage Dying Process was first presented to the world in Kubler-Ross's work, *On Death and Dying*. It has since appeared in countless periodicals, from *Good Housekeeping* to *The American Journal of Psychiatry*. The stages leading to the good death are: Denial, Anger, Bargaining, Depression, and Acceptance.

Kubler-Ross believes these stages occur chronologically, although she carefully deflects the criticism that she tied dying to a sequential procrustean bed. In *On Death and Dying* she notes that her stages should not be viewed too rigidly, yet she then proceeds to spell them out in a consecutive fashion, chapter by chapter. She is more aware of her critics in her second book. "I hope," she writes, "that I am making it clear that patients do not necessarily follow a classical pattern from the stage of denial to the stage of anger, to bargaining, to depression and acceptance. Most of my patients have exhibited two or three stages simultaneously and these do not always occur in the same order."[2] With the general acceptance of her stage theory, however, Kubler-Ross attaches no qualification to her myth. In her book *Living with Death and Dying* (1981), she notes that most of her patients go through five chronological stages which she proceeds to enumerate.

Ironically, even if Kubler-Ross were to announce the fluid nature of her stages on a nationally televised talk show, it would make little difference to the public's understanding. When it comes to scientific ideas, our tendency is to concretize and specify, whether or not this was the intent of the discoverer. This process is not unique to the myth under consideration. Louis Pasteur had no sooner shown that germs caused disease than others trumpeted the "fact" that science could isolate the organisms causing cancer, multiple sclerosis, and a number of maladies whose causes are yet unknown. Within a year after Rudolf Virchow demonstrated the power of microscopic pathology, supporters were stating that brain lesions for suicidal behavior could be named. Even false ideas have been dogmatized and developed. In 1903 M. René Blondlot, a distinguished physicist, claimed to have discovered a mysterious N-ray. Shortly thereafter followers described many amazing properties of the N-ray that Blondlot had not imagined. Two years after his discovery the N-ray disappeared from scientific literature. Apparently it had never existed. For many, the chronology of the Five Stage Dying Process is written in stone, and often the final stage of the sequence is invested with more magical properties than the creator of the myth may have envisioned.

In order to understand the stage theory, we must describe its component parts. Let me note at the outset that Kubler-Ross's hypothesis is a progressive conception. Each stage is a bit more positive than the one before it, because it brings the individual closer to an acceptance of his terminality. The first "adjustment reaction"[3] to the news of the terminal illness is denial. At this initial juncture, the patient may reject the physician's diagnosis. Kubler-Ross writes: "Denial functions as a buffer after unexpected shocking news, allows the patient to collect himself and, with time, mobilize the other, less radical defenses."[4]

The second stage through which the terminally ill patient passes is anger. Again this is a better adjustment to bad news. The "No, not me"[5] is replaced by "Why me?"[6] as the reality of dying begins to dawn. According to Kubler-Ross, anger is vented primarily at the healthy individual who the patient now regards enviously.

The third stage of the dying process is bargaining. The patient moves from hostility to a "Yes, it's me, but"[7] attitude. He acknowledges the reality of his situation, but attempts to circumvent or postpone death. Bargaining usually takes place between the patient and God. The individual promises to dedicate himself to the church or a worthy cause if God will cure his disease or allow him an extension of time. Kubler-Ross notes that the bargaining stage is more hopeful than the other two, and that it is often mistaken for the final stage of acceptance.

When physical deterioration makes it evident that a miracle will not happen, the patient moves from bargaining to depression. Kubler-Ross distinguishes between two types, reactive depression in which the patient mourns past losses, and preparatory grief in which he mourns the loss of his future, including his life. In the fourth stage, the individual begins to wean himself away from everything that might prevent him from dying the good death.

Depression leads to the final stage, acceptance. According to Kubler-Ross, acceptance is a summing up of the individual's life, a time "when he will contemplate his end with a certain degree of quiet expectation."[8] The individual pulls into himself and floats peacefully toward death. In *On Death and Dying* Kubler-Ross notes that acceptance should not be mistaken for a happy state. "It is almost devoid of feelings."[9] Yet her own idea of acceptance goes through stages of development. In her second book, *Questions and Answers on Death and Dying* (1974), Kubler-Ross writes that people who reach the acceptance stage "show a very outstanding feeling of equanimity and peace. There is something very dignified about these people."[10] In 1978 she states that those who enter the final stage will "emerge from the struggle with the radiance of a jewel."[11] By 1979 she says in an interview that acceptance "is the most beautiful experience you will have."[12] Indeed, along with the prophet's, a nation's thinking evolved in a positive direction. Not long ago, at a death and dying seminar I was conducting, a woman asked me if the acceptance stage indicated that science had proved the religious concept of Nirvana. A friend who is cynical about the boom in doom literature wonders how Kubler-Ross will supersede her optimistic pronouncements in the next decade. "There is nowhere to go, but down," he notes.

In Kubler-Ross's thinking, the Five Stage Dying Process is a natural event which will occur if patients are allowed to die without interference. The basic problem is society's fear of death. Dying frightens the patient because we burden him with our own phobias about the end. Thus family members, for example, may refuse to talk to an individual about his disease when he is ready to open up. Or health professionals—who want to rid themselves of bad news—may discuss a patient's death when he is still in the stage of denial. Because of his own fear, a doctor may attempt to resuscitate an individual who, floating in the stage of acceptance, does not want to be rescued. Kubler-Ross's books are filled with anecdotes of how patients are psychologically booby-trapped by well meaning, but frightened supporters. If we can come to terms with our own death-denying fears, notes the good doctor, we will be able to help the patient die a good death.

Scientific Problems

Although Kubler-Ross's theory claims to be scientific, we must question its empiric value. The first problem is that the Swiss psychiatrist's analysis lacks the methodological precision demanded by researchers. The background for *On Death and Dying* is a case study in which she interviewed two hundred or so dying patients. Not in that book or in subsequent volumes are we privy to the criteria she used to obtain her results. What questions, for example, were asked to determine whether a patient's statement reflected anger or depression? What was the standardized time frame devoted to each patient? We are given no statistics, no control groups—nothing, in short, which comprises scientific method as it is conventionally understood. In 1977 Robert Kastenbaum, one of the leading authorities in the field, wrote: "For the better part of a decade, then, the basic stage conceptualization has been taken on faith."[13]

This in itself would not be insuperable if research confirmed Kubler-Ross's hypothesis. Einstein, for example, postulated the Theory of Relativity long before physicists had the technical know-how to prove it. This is not the case with the Swiss psychiatrist's work. Research indicates that the stage theory is not an accurate reflection of the dying process. Scientists have noted that Kubler-Ross's stages may be components of phases in the dying process, but that they cannot be viewed in any kind of chronological order. Expressing the consensus, death expert Edwin Shneidman writes:

> Indeed, while I have seen in dying persons isolation, envy, bargaining, depression, and acceptance, I do not believe that these are necessarily "stages" of the dying process, and I am not at all convinced that they are lived through in that order, or, for that matter, in any universal order. What I do see is a complicated clustering of intellectual and effective states, some fleeting, lasting for a moment of a day or a week, set, not unexpectedly, against the backdrop of that person's total personality, his "philosophy of life."[14]

Instead of stages, researchers have found that one aspect of Kubler-Ross's theory may be the dominant pattern to an individual's dying. Studies have shown that denial and depression are important psychological factors through the course of terminal illness.[15] Conspicuously absent from the research is the idea that acceptance is a universal part of a dying person's makeup. In an important study on terminally ill patients, Charles Garfield noted that only 5 to 10 per cent of those hospitalized reached what we would term the acceptance stage.[16]

Another problem with the Swiss psychiatrist's research is that it fails to take into account a number of important variables. Kastenbaum, Kalish, and Garfield,[17] among others, have noted that the Five Stage Dying Process seems immune to sex and age differences, ethnicity, and personality traits of individual patients. Although Kubler-Ross provides biographical information about patients she interviews, the reader soon understands that it has no bearing on the formation of stages. In her hands, the individual, whatever his background, is simply part of a homogenous grouping.

The psychiatrist also fails to evaluate differences in disease and how this variable affects her model. Those dying of multiple sclerosis are lumped with those dying of cancer; those whose hospital stay is lengthy are melded with those whose tenure is brief. In *On Death and Dying,* the variety of causes of death is unimportant to her understanding of dying, an assumption few thanatologists would make. Finally Kubler-Ross fails to factor in the effect of drugs on the terminally ill person's understanding of death. Isn't it probable that powerful euphoriants like Brompton's Cocktail diminish the objectivity of a patient's response? Kubler-Ross thinks not. In order to maintain that the five stages is an objective and natural process, she must discount the idea that drugs have tainted her findings.

Another problem with the psychiatrist's model is that it is difficult to pinpoint her stages. Although I have dealt with the terminally ill for more than twelve years, I have yet to identify stages within people I visit. When I compare my observations with other helping professionals, I find that none of us can agree on a particular stage of a particular patient.

I am not unique. In an interesting study, Dr. George Fitchett, a chaplain and professor at the Rush

Presbyterian–St. Luke's Medical Center in Chicago, conducted a survey among experienced and inexperienced raters. They were given a verbatim interview and asked to assess the overall emotional status of the patient. The source of the report was the case of Mr. G., an illustration of acceptance in Kubler-Ross's initial work. The results of Dr. Fitchett's test are interesting. Every stage in the theory was selected by at least one rater as the best description of the patient's outlook. While the greatest number of raters agreed with Kubler-Ross that the patient showed signs of acceptance, an almost equal number said that the patient evidenced denial, the stage at the opposite end of the spectrum. Ironically two-thirds of the *experienced* raters viewed Mr. G's state in terms of denial![18] That most of us guess at stages leads me to believe they are more fiction than fact.

The myth of the Five Stage Dying Process collapses under scientific scrutiny. Even if research supported Kubler-Ross's theory, however, there would still be problems interpreting the meaning of those stages. George Kuykendall, a minister and professor at Fordham University, has shown that the five adjustment reactions, as they are reported by their discoverer, indicate psychic regression rather than development. Viewing Kubler-Ross's work along classic psychoanalytic lines, Kuykendall notes that the movement from denial to anger, for example, is a step in a negative direction, since the kind of anger that Kubler-Ross describes indicates greater ego breakdown, a greater distance from reality, than the denial stage. Thus down the psychic road to death, acceptance, as the Swiss psychiatrist defines it, is not the highest, but the lowest stage. "Common sense asks why the last stage is called acceptance," Kuykendall writes. "The behavior described seems more like exhaustion and depletion; the individual is too drained by sickness, medical treatments, and hopelessness to feel anything very strongly....Psychoanalytically, the final stage is understood as the complete collapse of all mature psychological function. Individuals retreat into the passivity of earliest infancy and manifest little involvement in anything beyond their own discomforts and feelings."[19] Kuykendall rightly understands that to talk about a progressive stage theory in which the ultimate goal is infantilism is to talk about an absurdity.

If the Five Stage Dying Process is not the result of scientific observation, one wonders how the concept originated. With the help of Glen Davidson, a former associate of Kubler-Ross, let me relate the birth of the present myth. One of Elisabeth's colleagues at the Billings Hospital in Chicago was a brilliant student named Carl Nighswonger. Nighswonger interned as a chaplain at the M. D. Anderson Cancer Center in Houston. While there he read an article that described how patients adjust to prostheses. The author noted that amputees go through a four stage adaptive process: denial, anger, depression, and acceptance. When Nighswonger returned to Chicago, he brought the stage theory with him and applied it to the terminally ill. He and Kubler-Ross added a middle stage, bargaining, and *voila!*, a myth was born. Thus the origin of the Five Stage Dying Process had little to do with careful observation of terminally ill patients.

Practical Problems

Not only is the myth under consideration theoretically bankrupt; it also complicates the dying process. The test of any faith is not its scientific verifiabilty, but whether it works in the trenches of life—and death. The Five Stage Dying Process fails in these respects. Using several examples, let me discuss the problems it causes the dying patient, and then turn to problems it causes loved ones.

Max

In his late sixties, Max was a towering man who had been a sheet metal worker before his retirement. A widower, he lived alone in a small town before the cancer of the pancreas diagnosis. I knew him a little less than two months before he died. Max's problem involved an attractive young nurse who had befriended him. On a number of occasions, he talked about her kindness and added once with a wink, that she must have a crush on him. One day he failed to mention her name, and I sensed the relationship had soured. Somewhat later Max noted that the nurse had asked him to confide in her so that she could help him "progress" through his dying. He asked her what she meant, and she explained the lore of Kubler-Ross. Her conversation had a negative impact on the patient. Max believed that she viewed him more as a guinea pig than a friend, and he resented her initial play for his friendship. Unfortunately, as Max learned more about the five stage theory, he began to believe his response to cancer was atypical. He had not denied the seriousness of his condition nor was he angry at the world for his lot. He became burdened with the idea that he was dying incorrectly, that his behavior was abnormal, that, as he put it, he was "off the track." Thus, for Max, the pressure to die in a prescribed manner added another load to his overtaxed psyche.

Having met the nurse on several occasions, I realized her attempt to play thanatologist arose from concern for her patients. Unfortunately her zeal was misguided. Let me add, too, that families and friends also tried to help the patient by informing him of the nature of the good death. Such news, as we have seen, is often not helpful.

Geri

Another problem with the myth is exemplified by the case of Geri. A thirty-two-year-old mother of two, she was diagnosed as having multiple sclerosis a year before I met her in the hospital. She had gone to graduate school and stopped in the middle of a Ph.D. program in order to marry and start a family. In our talks about dying she manifested knowledge of the stage theory. Although she dreaded the loss of her family, she expressed no fear of dying personally. Her end, she believed, would be peaceful. One evening I received a call from Geri's husband, asking me to visit her in the hospital. When I arrived, Geri was very weak and believed death was near. Dispensing with small talk, she grabbed my hand. "So I die easily," she said. After a brief pause, she added, "So what?" She was experiencing what one psychologist describes as *ego chill*, "a shudder which comes from the sudden awareness that our nonexistence is entirely possible."[20]

Geri's room was indescribably "cold" that evening. She realized that even if she reached a stage of acceptance, this in itself could not remove her primal fear. Had she been duped into believing it would? she wondered. Although Geri was not religious, she told me once that her conception of an afterlife was colored by her father's job, plumbing. She thought resurrection meant that her particles would dissolve in the water table, and she would live on as drink for plants. During her dark night of the soul, however, she needed greater hope to sustain her.

The myth of the Five Stage Dying Process complicates

the end of life. The terminally ill patient is given a mandate to die in a certain way. Anxiety is produced when he doesn't measure up to the Kubler-Ross standard imposed by those around him. The myth also offers to banish our fear of death. This it cannot do, for man's fear of death is rooted in his dread of nonexistence, a problem that is not touched by the blissful nature of one's demise. Not only is the myth problematic for the dying, it also tangles the lives of those who stand at bedside. Janet and Tom are two individuals whose stories illustrate the problems for survivors.

Janet

I first met Janet after her son died. The funeral director had given her my name, and she dropped by to make final arrangements. At age twenty-eight her son Scott had lost the battle to bone cancer. His had been an especially painful and debilitating case. A couple of months before he died, Janet had been advised by a friend to attend a death and dying workshop in a nearby city. There she learned of Kubler-Ross and the stage theory. She derived hope from the fact that Scott would reach a stage of acceptance where he would be at peace. The naturalness of the myth impressed her. Janet and her husband owned a farm and, from their observation of animals, they believed dying was as natural as birth. Janet returned from the seminar and disseminated her findings to her husband and Scott's two brothers. Throughout the final weeks they waited for nature to take its course.

Scott never made the fifth stage. He died with pain and fear, conditions the family had not expected. Janet's sorrow was compounded by self-blame. At the seminar, she learned that the patient's family can help facilitate the dying process. Although she thought she had helped

Scott in every way, apparently she had not. Thus she came to arrange a funeral, and confess to me that she had failed her son when he needed her most. Scott did not reach acceptance because of her. Although I tried, I could not dislodge the legacy of guilt the myth bequeathed her.

Tom

Tom, a close friend and parishioner, struggled with his father's dying. Near the end, the son tried to convince himself that his father had reached the acceptance stage. From what I could see, acceptance was temporary and induced by morphine. His father spent his final week drifting in and out of pain. One Saturday Tom left his parent's bedside midmorning to spend time with his wife and children. I, too, visited his father that day and, sensing the end was near, returned in the evening. God often lets us appear at crucial junctures in people's lives. This was one of them. Not more than five minutes before I arrived, Tom had entered his father's room and found him dead—propped on his elbows with an expression of terror stamped on his face. Having consigned his father to the fifth stage, he was unprepared for the grotesque visage that greeted him. Tom blamed himself for misdiagnosing his father's stage. If he hadn't left that morning, he might have helped his father from depression to acceptance.

I find most people feel guilty when a loved one dies. They could have done more for the individual while he was alive. They could have been kinder, more attentive. Although guilt is normal under the circumstances, it is magnified by belief in the Five Stage Dying Process. If dying is naturally positive, then the only reason for someone to die badly is that he has been tainted by the exponents of a death-denying society. The onus is not on the nature of death itself, but rather on the insensitivity of loved ones and support groups. The guilt produced by the myth is unwarranted.

Why We Believe

Although the myth of the Five Stage Dying Process is theoretically bankrupt, and practically dangerous, it does serve as a palliative for the healthy. The myth imposes order on a mysterious and terrifying event. It is our attempt to quantify the unquantifiable. By reducing the dying experience to five neat stages, we buy the illusion that man's knowledge has tamed the Grim Reaper. This accounts for the popularity of a number of death-stage theories besides the work of Kubler-Ross.[21] Indeed the myth insulates us from the reality of dying by providing what surgeon Robert Hudson calls the "cookbook approach" to terminality. He writes:

> Here are five stages, and a remedy for each. Repressed anger stage? Tear down all the get-well cards or throw a ball point pen at the next devil who walks through the door. Depression stage? Merely point out that it is normal to be depressed at the thought of dying, that if you were in their fix, you would be depressed also; besides take heart, the depressed phase comes just before acceptance, so all will soon be well.[22]

With Kubler-Ross as our reference, we need not confront the unique problems a dying patient faces. We have reduced him to a type, whose ending yields to standard, facile answers. There is great irony here, for Kubler-Ross has maintained that the dying should be our teachers. The effect of her stage theory is just the opposite. By imposing a model on their experience, we become schoolmarms in their classroom. It is a safer role for us than that of student.

Perhaps, too, in a deeper sense, the myth attracts because it orders time in general. In our post-Christian era writers and philosophers correctly inform us that without God, time is meaningless. This is especially true in Western society, derived as it is from a Judeo-Christian background. Today we no longer perceive special moments—salvation events—on the road of life. Indeed, we have trouble perceiving the road itself. Perhaps the most important and widely read existential novel of our era begins by subverting the linear nature of time itself. Camus opens *The Stranger* with these sentences:

> Mother died today. Or, maybe, yesterday: I cannot be sure. The telegram from the Home says: YOUR MOTHER PASSED AWAY. FUNERAL TOMORROW. DEEP SYMPATHY. Which leaves the matter doubtful; it could have been yesterday.[23]

Calling time "drifting wreckage," the poet T. S. Eliot writes: "the way up is the way down, the way forward is the way back."[24] The meaningless nature of time is reinforced by the media. Our newspapers, televisions, and radios bombard us with Eternal Now: We are told that the legion of events, which parade daily before us in mind-numbing rapidity, are of utmost importance; yet everything is forgotten and discarded by the media in the wake of a new day's happenings. History is seen as useless as a week-old newspaper. Adrift in the protean nature of the present, we have lost the ability to pick out crucial moments in history—ours as well as the world's.

If everything is important, then, truly, nothing is. Noting secular man's time dilemma, theologian Nathan Scott writes:

> So, since the tempo of human life in our period leads men to experience time as scattered and fluid, inevitably there arises the anxious surmise that there may be nothing any longer that can be counted on to hold time together, to order it and stabilize it and give it firm anchorage. Which is to say that Eternity is felt to be in eclipse.[25]

In the past, the Bible made time coherent for Christian cultures. The individual saw his society mirrored in the biblical drama of Israel, which proceeded in a linear fashion from one important event to the next. Then, too, he saw his life in the lives of biblical characters— lives ordered from birth to death by the will of God. In our post-Christian age myths like the Five Stage Dying Process substitute for the Bible. Kubler-Ross's theory gives time meaning—albeit a brief span. There are signposts, five salvation events to be exact, on the short road to terminality. The consequences of the Swiss psychiatrist's thinking go beyond dying itself, for her work spawned a variety of stage theories to account for the totality of one's life. Books like Gail Sheehy's *Passages* tell us far more about our need to make sense out of history than they do about "typical" stages of an individual's life.

While the myth is attractive because it breaks dying into predictable stages, it is downright seductive in its claim that dying is blissful. Kubler-Ross's idea fits a culture that subsumes all experience under the pleasure principle. Since the sixties there has been a growing tendency to translate the drug high into a variety of activities. Americans have joined cults that regulate their eating, sleeping, and waking activities; devotees willingly surrender adulthood for the security of infancy. Abandoning religion that calls for involvement with reality, Americans increasingly join churches that equate salvation with drug-like euphoria. Many embrace therapies in which they float in contraptions that purportedly duplicate the womb, or "bliss out" in pillow-bedecked rooms. We are addicted to television and computer games because they hypnotize; we are jogging junkies because of the endorphin high it brings. We spend millions on rock bands who numb our senses with phantasmagoric displays of light and sound. The list goes on.

Writing about modern composers, Richard Sennett notes: "Respite—this is what the best music offers. It is perhaps a terrible sadness that the conditions of daily existence in our civilization are such that people feel compelled to 'relax' by dropping into a trance, rather than enjoying the various rhythms of their days."[26] Senett's comment about music is applicable to any number of activities in our society. Indeed, when we view Kubler-Ross's acceptance stage in its cultural context, we realize that it is not a definition of dying so much as it is a description of good living as viewed by many Americans.

In Aldous Huxley's novel *Brave New World*, Mustapha Mond, who sounds like a disciple of Kubler-Ross, confronts a romantic known as the Savage. Mond states:

> "We prefer to do things comfortably."
> "But I don't want comfort. I want God, I want poetry. I want real danger, I want freedom, I want goodness. I want sin."
> "In fact, " said Mustapha Mond, "you're claiming the right to be unhappy."

"All right then," said the Savage defiantly, "I'm claiming the right to be unhappy."[27]

We cannot romanticize the past the way Huxley does through the character of the Savage. Earlier peoples would not have affirmed the "right to unhappiness" any more than people today. Nevertheless living in an earlier Christian culture, Everyman would have found more kinship with the Savage than with the pleasure-demanding modern, Mond. A pain-free existence, Everyman realized, was not part of his birthright. Pain was accepted and, with biblical aid, transcended. The Bible comforted Everyman for several reasons. First, it showed him that he didn't suffer alone. When he viewed the biblical account, he realized that pain was endemic to the children of Israel, God's chosen, and to the Lord himself. Second, Everyman realized that people's faith grew in the face of pain. Job's communion with God deepened at the end of his struggle. Everyman could learn of God through his own anguish. Third, in the resurrection of Jesus Christ, Everyman saw God transform suffering into hope. The Bible thus taught him to look to the immediate future for a sudden turnaround in his own fortune. Finally, and most important, faith in the New Jerusalem helped him to relativize suffering. Pain might be protracted; nevertheless, in the time frame of eternal life, its importance diminished. In spite of "the slings and arrows of outrageous fortune," he knew his inheritance awaited him in heaven. Because of his faith, Everyman could accept pain as a part of life.

In a post-Christian world, secular Everyman has no God to make sense out of pain, let alone transform it. Therefore pain is senseless. Instead of understanding it, he can only try to remove it. Salvation for secular man is an absence of pain, a moment of bliss, before the lights go out. As the case of Geri illustrates, and as we shall see in the following section, such hope cannot assuage his fear of dying.

Biblical Considerations

The Bible does not indicate that people die in stages. Nowhere is there a pattern we can discern. This is true of the most important death in the Bible, that of Jesus Christ. If God wanted to stress the Five Stage Dying Process, he could have done so at Golgotha. Still, some have tried to find dying order in our Lord's demise. Jesus reaches the acceptance stage in Luke and John, it is maintained. This cannot be, however, since acceptance, as it is defined by Kubler-Ross, means a turning into oneself. But in these accounts, Jesus manifests responsible involvement with others, not infantilism. Moments before he dies in Luke's gospel, he tells the repentant thief that he will join the Son of Man in Paradise and in the gospel of John Jesus entrusts his mother to the care of his beloved disciple.

Even if Jesus' psychological state could be described as acceptance in the third and fourth Evangelists, God throws a monkey wrench into our calculations with the other two accounts. In Matthew and Mark, Jesus' life ends with these words: "My God, My God, why have You forsaken Me?" Some commentators downplay the cry of dereliction by noting that he may have been quoting Psalm 22, a hymn that ends on a triumphant note. This idea finds no explicit support from the Evangelists themselves, however; there is, in other words, no attempt to sugarcoat those terrible words. In the four Gospels, then, enough ambiguity exists to avoid falling into the stage-setting trap. That Jesus' dying defies analysis can be seen in the attempts of later Christians to break it down into religious stages. Pious renderings of the Stations of the Cross and accounts of the "Seven Last Words of Jesus" show our discomfort with the open-ended nature of the Passion.

In the same manner, the Bible does not support the idea that dying is naturally blissful. Although there is no attempt to turn biblical heroes into Stoics by detailing physiological and psychological distress, nevertheless there is an underlying assumption that pain may be part of one's ending. Certainly this is the message we receive from Jesus' death. If God wanted to illustrate a final euphoric stage, he could have put his Son in the position of Socrates, drinking hemlock among friends in surroundings more conducive to the idea than Golgotha. The Son of Man meets his death on a torture instrument of such horror that ancient sources are loath to describe it. Seneca, a Roman statesman and contemporary of St. Paul, comments tersely: "Can anyone be found who would prefer wasting away in pain, dying limb by limb, or letting out his life drop by drop, rather than by expiring once for all?"[28]

In 1968 a team of archaeologists uncovered the remains of someone who had been crucified, the first and only such discovery. The man was in his midtwenties and came from a well-to-do Jewish family. He had a cleft palate and sported a full beard. His name was Yehohanon, the son of Hagakol, and he may have shared the same time frame as Jesus. From the angle of the nail through his heel bones, scholars discovered that Yehohanon's knees were drawn up near the chest, in an excruciating flex position. What his remains revealed to scientists was that crucifixion was far more painful than they had imagined. Added to the physical torment was the psychological agony of dying on a public thoroughfare before an indifferent, if not hostile audience. Even if Jesus had not uttered those terrible words recorded in the first two gospels, his manner of execution militates against the idea that dying is naturally blissful.

The Bible, at least by example, indicates that death is neither ordered nor euphoric. In fact dying is a terrifying prospect because humans perceive death as an enemy, an implacable foe against whom man struggles. Why is this so? Because we were created in God's image, the Bible tells us, he has endowed us with certain innate characteristics. Chief among them is our hunger for eternal life. "He has put eternity in their hearts," the author of Ecclesiastes states (3:11). Death, then, stands as an unnatural roadblock to our divine programming. Although Freud denied the existence of God, he nevertheless understood that death flies in the face of what we know about ourselves instinctively. He could write, after observing the carnage of World War I: "It is indeed impossible to imagine our own death; and whenever we attempt to do so, we can perceive that we are, in fact, still present as spectators."[29]

Freud's view has been echoed by many others. Death expert Avery Weisman follows the father of psychoanalysis and then goes a step further in the right direction: "Man accepts the reality of organic and objective death, but cannot imagine his own extinction," he writes. "Consequently despite obvious depletion and deterioration, most patients still cling to an image of survival which promises to preserve their unique, distinctive consciousness."[30] His latter point has been confirmed in my work with the dying. Near the end of life, the questions a terminally ill patient asks are these: "Will I survive my death?" "Will I meet dead loved ones?" "Will I find God?"

Can you see why the myth of the Five Stage Dying Process fails? To die blissfully means nothing to people who believe their destiny is eternal life. Humans can adapt to physical and psychological distress if they know that nonexistence does not await them.

A final question must be asked before I close this chapter. If our purpose is to spend eternity with God, why is there death in the first place? Let me give a brief answer. When Paul tells us that death is the result of man's sin (see Rom. 6:23), he is writing primarily about Adam's transgression. The first man violated God's command by eating the fruit of the Tree of Good and Evil. The reason for his action goes beyond hunger and rebellion. The serpent informed him that in eating, "Your eyes will be opened, and you will be like God, knowing good and evil"(Gen. 3:5). Although God had warned him that death would be his punishment if he ate, Adam did so in order to become God himself. Mortality was imposed upon him as a grim reminder that he was a creature, and not the Creator. Adam's finitude was impressed upon him with God's final words of judgment: "For dust you are, and to dust you shall return"(Gen. 3:19).

Although death is the consequence of sin, a terrible reality which the Bible does not whitewash, there is a positive purpose in its design. For in giving an eternal *no* to man's divine pretensions, it forces him to put his trust in someone other than the Unholy Trinity: Me, Myself, and I. We may spend our lives playing God, wheeling and dealing, dictating to others how they are to behave. We may command armies and navies and have the world at our feet. There comes a time, however, when all of our power is useless, and we cannot control our own lives, let alone the destiny of the world. There comes a time when we cannot save ourselves from what we fear most—the thought of nonexistence. Dying forces us to acknowledge our dependency on a force greater than ourselves for salvation from fear. Dying forces us to acknowledge God.

Our task as Christians is to help the terminally ill patient to see the Great Other in his midst, as he journeys toward death. He needs to be reminded of the hope that may be buried beneath the rubble of his secularism: that he is a child of God whose purpose is to commune eternally with his Maker and Redeemer.

5

The Myth of the Near Death Experience

The second major myth with which I shall deal is the "Near Death Experience." Like the Five Stage Dying Process it disguises the nature of death behind a progressive stage theory whose end result is bliss. In the Near Death Experience, however, the high is achieved out of the body. The importance of this theory is that, on the surface, it seems to answer the theological problem I raised in the previous chapter. "Yes, we are immortal," the myth assures us. "One need not worry since death is simply a euphoric transition from one life to the next."

In his initial work, *Life After Life,* Dr. Raymond Moody notes that people who come close to dying share common afterlife experiences. Although he mentions fifteen aspects, he focuses on six sequential stages. The first impression is sound. The auditory sensation is heightened, and the moribund patient feels surrounded by music or noise. One woman heard Japanese wind bells, "tingling a long way off."[1]

The second impression is movement through a dark tunnel or trough. The individual experiences a rapid pulling away from self, a feeling, as one patient described, akin to "riding on a roller coaster train at an amusement park."[2]

The out-of-body phase is the third stage of the dying process. At this point the patient realizes he is floating above the "corpse" in the bed or on the operating table. He observes efforts to resuscitate himself and discovers that in his new spiritual body he can pass through walls, doors, and other material objects. While this is a blissful state, there is a tinge of loneliness because he cannot communicate with those he sees.

This problem is solved in the fourth stage, when the psychic voyager meets other spiritual entities who assure him that all is well. One woman noted:

> They were all people I had known in my past life, but who had passed on before. I recognized my grandmother and a girl I had known when I was in school, and many other relatives and friends. It seems that I mainly saw their faces and felt their presence. They all seemed pleased. It was a very happy occasion, and I felt that they had come to protect or guide me. It was almost as if I were coming home, and they were there to greet or welcome me. All this time, I had the feeling of everything light and beautiful. It was a beautiful and glorious moment.[3]

The glorious moment reaches its climax when the individual spies a ball of light that gradually increases in brightness. This force is far from impersonal as Moody describes it:

> ...not one person has expressed any doubt whatsoever that it was a being, a being of light. Not only that, it is a personal being. It has a very definite personality. The love and warmth which emanate from this being to the dying person are utterly beyond words, and he feels

completely surrounded by it and taken up in it, completely at ease and accepted in the presence of this being. He senses an irresistible attraction to this light. He is ineluctably drawn to it.[4]

Nirvana is achieved at this point. The being of light asks the individual questions about the meaning of his life and then conducts an all-encompassing review in which the patient's history passes before him in a vivid, kaleidoscopic fashion. According to Moody, this being conforms to the individual's religious or philosophical understanding. Some believe the light is Christ or God; others think it is a special angel or a messenger.

The sixth stage is anticlimatic. The individual is escorted to a border he cannot pass and then returns to his body where he rejoins the living.

Like Kubler-Ross, who, incidentally, writes the introduction to *Life After Life*, Moody makes a half-hearted attempt to qualify his findings. The stages should not be taken too literally, he notes. Having warned us, he proceeds to lay out the phases in a sequential pattern and even presents us with a picture of what the typical dying process entails. Moody also hedges in another area. At the beginning of his book he notes that he is not trying to prove immortality. There may be other reasons that explain the phenomena he observes. Nevertheless he easily dismisses divergent views, preferring instead to dwell on similarities between the Near Death Experience and accounts of immortality found in Plato, the eighteenth century mystic Swedenborg, and the writings of Tibetan monks. His findings, one readily infers, validate future life.

Although Moody's study was considered groundbreaking by the public, his brand of inquiry has antecedents. In 1882 the Society for Psychical Research was formed in England by scientists and philosophers who believed Darwinism had eroded the credibility of religion. A primary aim of the organization was to give immortality scientific underpinnings. Thus a voluminous amount of anecdotal material was collected and catalogued. One of the most famous life-after-death cases typifies the stories that appeared in monographs and articles. In 1921 Chaffin Will, a North Carolina farmer, died and left his estate to his third son, disinheriting his older sons and wife. After the funeral Will appeared to his son James. The young man was instructed to search his father's overcoat. What James discovered was a scrap of paper which directed him to an old family Bible. In it, marking the twenty-seventh chapter of Genesis (Jacob steals his elder brother's birthright), was a second will which divided Chaffin's estate equally among his heirs. A court later upheld the legality of this document.

Generally research involved those who saw apparitions of deceased family members and friends, but it soon dawned on parapsychologists that it was more scientific to collect stories of people who had "died" and returned to life. In 1892 a physician named Albert Heim studied thirty mountaineers who took life-threatening falls in the Alps. Heim noted: "There was no anxiety, no trace of despair, no pain; but rather calm seriousness, profound acceptance, and a dominant mental quickness and sense of surety."[5] Heim did not speculate on immortality, but later researchers did. Studies by James Hyslop (1919) and William Barrett (1926) explored the deathbed vision and its implications for future life. By 1930 interest in immortality waned, and parapsychologists turned their attention to ESP and other psychic manifestations.

It was not until 1961 that the issue was revived in Karlis Osis's book, *Deathbed Observations by Patients and Nurses.* Osis mailed questionnaires to thousands of helping professionals, then performed a computer analysis on the responses. His findings anticipated Moody's, although the out-of-body phase and the mysterious being of light are conspicuously absent. Unlike Moody, Osis did not "stage" his results, the theoretical linchpin that insured the latter's public success. Much of Moody's work, then, builds on the parapsychic foundations laid during the closing decade of the nineteenth century, although his sequential ordering of the experience is unique.

Scientific Problems

While parapsychic research is extremely interesting, it garners little support from the scientific community. How does one verify excursions into immortality? Certainly the scientist cannot go along on the psychic voyager's ride. Then, too, the language used to describe such experiences does not lend itself to empirical analysis, since few can even describe what has happened to them. Like Christian statements of the resurrection, Moody's accounts must be taken on faith.

Apart from methodological considerations, there are other problems that militate against the scientific nature of Moody's enterprise. Even if the phenomena he records could be measured empirically, his conclusion does not fit his data. Moody tells the reader that no two dying experiences are alike, and that, in fact, no single account has all the components of the Near Death Experience. In some examples, we see that even important segments like the tunnel and the being of light are missing. Thus the model he proposes does not reflect his findings.

A second problem is that he derives his results from disparate data. Although he writes about dying experiences, Moody nevertheless includes accounts of people who were neither ill nor injured. The individual whose life flashes before him as he avoids a car crash is one example. Lumping this experience with a patient who survives serious surgery is like measuring oranges in terms of apples. A third problem is that his definition of dying is too vague. In a model of linguistic imprecision, Moody notes that he interviewed some "who were resuscitated after having been thought, adjudged, or pronounced clinically dead by their doctors."[6] Is there a difference, the reader wonders, between the patient who is "adjudged" dead, and one who is "pronounced" dead? We get no clear idea of the criteria Moody uses to define dying or death.

The fundamental problem with his research is that the phenomena he records have no bearing on the subject of afterlife, for although his patients may have been dying, they were not dead. From a scientific perspective, the accounts of "immortality" would have validity if someone returned from the grave and related his experience. Moody tries to cloud the issue by noting that his patients were "clinically dead." He means certain physiological signs such as pulse, respiration, and pupillary contraction in the presence of light ceased for a brief period. Of course these people were not dead, since their vital signs were restored. Indeed one can argue that none of Moody's patients were as close to the end as an individual who lies in an irreversible coma because the neocortex of his brain (where consciousness and personality are embedded) has been destroyed. Physicians rarely talk of death as a cessation of vital signs. Rather terminality is viewed in terms of the critical period after heart and respiration stop and brain cells begin to die from lack of oxygen and glucose. Moody's cases have not suffered brain damage, let alone death, therefore his phrase "clinically dead" is especially misleading.

While the findings of *Life After Life* may tell us something about the experiences of dying, they do not prove the existence of an afterlife. Dr. Ian Stevenson, the only physician I know whose work on the Near Death Experience filled an issue of a leading medical journal, could write: "...the published reports of close encounters with death have not contributed anything to the objective evidence of the survival of the human personality after death."[7]

Scientists have shown that the Near Death Experience is similar to other phenomena that can be tested in a laboratory. The most extensive work on hallucinations has been done by Ronald K. Siegel, a research psychologist at the University of California at Los Angeles. Siegel notes that the state Moody describes can be reproduced in patients by certain hallucinatory drugs. The noise, the tunnel, out-of-body experiences, and encounters with spiritual entities are descriptions given by LSD and PCP users.[8] Some of the accounts Siegel records are almost identical to those found in *Life After Life*. The phenomena Moody describes are not related to afterlife, but rather to altered states of consciousness produced by variable stimuli. Surgeons have known for years that patients under anesthesia describe visions akin to the Near Death Experience. They also know that supposedly anesthetized patients can often hear conversation and sense movement that they later attribute to an out-of-body experience. Not long ago, an anesthesiologist advised: "Ideally conversation during surgery should be discreet, both in topic and sound level. Frivolity and storytelling with raucous laughter should be taboo, and earplugs should be considered when there is a history of awareness."[9]

The Near Death Experience is found, however, in those who are neither drugged nor seriously ill. Indeed it seems any number of stressful situations can trigger this reaction. Studies indicate that those who mourn the loss of a child or spouse often see a kaleidoscopic life review and experience an out-of-body state.[10] Other studies have shown similarities between the Near Death Experience and blissful states of the mystic and religious convert.[11]

Roy Kletti and Russell Noyes, of the University of Iowa's School of Medicine, see Moody's findings as a common reaction to stress of any sort. Faced with a problem, the individual will detach himself from his body, as it were, and study the situation from an objective distance. If stress is serious, the mind will construct an alternate world for itself which may be blissful as well as safe. The raw material for this world comes from one's personality and background. Thus the Near Death Experience by nature is too individual to stage as Moody has done. Kletti and Noyes conclude their study on depersonalized behavior by noting: "Single or unified interpretation of the subjective experiences during moments of life threatening danger is not available to us. Yet portrayed among the personal and moving accounts presented is the enormous adaptive capacity of the human mind."[12]

Practical Problems

Science cannot prove life after death, although it has explained the Near Death Experience in terms of hallucinations and psychological defense mechanisms. Nevertheless the popular belief that Moody's books confirms immortality complicates the problems of the patient and his family. Here are a few examples I have encountered:

Parker

At age thirty-nine Parker, an artist, entered the hospital for renal failure. During a particularly intense period in his treatment, he had what he considered a Near Death Experience. He heard noise which he described as a beating of wings amplified thousands of times. After a short journey through a winding cave, he was deposited on a cold, wind-blown desert. He began to walk toward a splotch of orange in a gray sky, thinking his movement toward light would bring warmth. The wind picked up, however, and he felt as if he were a human "window screen" in which every wire was chilled. In the distance he spied a dog he owned as a child, picking through a carcass. When he called the animal by name, it turned toward him and, in an instant, grew to enormous and threatening size. Parker tried to run, but the sand seemingly gripped his legs. The German shepherd attacked, crushing Parker in its jaws. The artist's last memory was viewing the bag of bones in the distance, and realizing it was himself.

The problem for Parker was that he was a deeply religious man who believed his nightmare was an excursion into the next world. He asked himself again and again what his experience meant theologically. He came to believe God was punishing him for a grave sin he had committed, and that if he had died that evening, he would have gone straight to hell. After his recovery, Parker spent fitful moments rummaging through his past, trying to uncover his great transgression. He came to me when he began losing his faith. He viewed God—if he existed—as a malevolent being who punished people for sins they could not discover. The Almighty played a cat and mouse game with his creation. Thus belief in the Near Death Experience tricked Parker into thinking that a departure from Moody's pattern indicated a deviant personality, one who is hopelessly at odds with God. Although I tried to assure him that many hallucinations were horrific, he did not believe he had been hallucinating. He had had a Near Death Experience. God had shown him hell.

Parker's case is interesting, but not unique. Others have recorded accounts that are directly opposite of the beatific versions amassed by Moody.[13] What we are attracted to, however, is Moody's particular vision of a future life.

Ted

Ted believed he had a Near Death Experience sometime during triple by-pass surgery. He experienced an out-of-body sensation and found himself drifting upward to what he thought was heaven. Sinking blissfully into a white cloud, he heard voices singing lullabies and, of all things, show tunes from the late thirties! Instead of a being of light, a headless angel in a white robe touched the top of his head with her hand. Ted remembers next struggling for life in the intensive care unit. Not a religious man, he came to see me at his wife's insistence. She hoped her husband's experience would make him a believer. Did it? I asked. Ted shook his head no, then added what others have since told me. As blissful as his out-of-body experience was, he did not fear death any less. In fact he became more squeamish. Shortly after his recovery, he and several buddies were watching a prize fight on television. When the battered boxer hit the canvas, Ted felt a sudden "stab of mortality" and left for the bathroom. "Whatever heaven is," Ted mentioned in my office, "it's not enough."

Although Moody leads the reader to believe that the Near Death Experience counteracts man's fear of death, my work indicates this is a partial truth. A positive psychic journey may complement one's faith in Christian resurrection, but it cannot serve as a substitute. In this regard, the findings of a recent Gallup Poll are interesting. The survey indicated that two-thirds of those who had a Near Death Experience still feared death.[14] Unfortunately the poll did not indicate other factors (e.g., religious belief) that may have affected the 33 per cent who believed the Near Death Experience diminished their fear.

Patrick

Patrick's situation represents the most common problem belief in the myth entails. A thirty-four-year-old funeral director, Patrick had a massive heart attack which permanently damaged the organ. There was nothing surgeons could do, and Patrick was left in a medical holding pattern. As a clergyman, I find coronary patients have unique problems. Surrounded by a ganglia of wires leading to monitors, there is a feeling in this electronic microcosm that one's life can end instantly. Nor is it comforting for the patient to be aware that he can chart his own demise on a computer screen measuring heart rate.

Patrick's work also complicated the picture. As a funeral director, he had been lulled into believing that dying was a mundane affair, not much to think or worry about. He was unprepared to find himself in the hospital, a place he routinely visited in the course of a week. To counteract his fear, Patrick focused on meditation techniques, and Raymond Moody. He had liberally dispensed *Life After Life* to the bereaved. Patrick was not religious, yet he believed his life would continue in some form. He also believed his dying would conform to Moody's pattern. He would be unconscious at death, his spirit having been whisked away to a future life before he knew what hit him. It was not to be. One evening I received a call from his wife, saying her husband was dying. Patrick's eyes, as I approached bedside, scanned his surroundings like luminescent radar trackers. His life was ending, and he realized no out-of-body experience was forthcoming. The story etched in his face and stenciled in his eyes was this: The placebo, the psychological sugar pill had not worked. A huge man, Patrick's heavy metal bed trembled with his fear.

The Near Death Experience also complicates the lives of those surrounding the patient. Like the Five Stage Dying Process, belief in this myth tricks people into thinking that dying is pain-free. Thus survivors are often shocked when a loved one's experience at the end is neither physiologically nor psychologically blissful. Faith in Moody's findings also throws a unique monkey wrench into the picture, as the following case illustrates.

Dorothy

Dorothy and Adam were in the midforties when he discovered he had a melanoma of the worst kind. Because their only child had died several year earlier, both had taken an interest in the death and dying movement. They viewed Moody's work as scientific confirmation of their religious belief. Adam's demise was of short duration and relatively pain-free. During the last two days of his life, he was comatose. For Dorothy, the problem was that she assumed Adam would regain consciousness and assure her of his destiny. She had been subtly conditioned by the accounts in *Life After Life* to think there would be a reawakening before death. After all, Moody's patients lived to tell their stories. Dorothy sat in my office one evening and said, "I thought for sure he'd come back and tell me about his parents and my daughter." Dorothy struggled theologically. Why hadn't God allowed Adam to communicate with her before he died, especially since he allowed other terminally ill patients that privilege? Had she sinned? Had Adam? Was his "abnormal" way of dying divine punishment? For Dorothy, belief in the Near Death Experience created more problems than it solved.

Why We Believe

Although belief in this myth complicates life for the patient and his family, it serves as a palliative for the healthy. Like the Five Stage Dying Process, it orders dying, reducing it to neat stages ending in bliss. The special appeal of the Near Death Experience is its religious veneer. It satisfies a society that desires the consolations of religion without paying religion's price. One can get by with the faith of Mrs. May, a character in Flannery O'Connor's short story "Greenleaf": "She was a good Christian woman with a large respect for religion, though she did not, of course, believe any of it was true."[15] According to *Life After Life*, heavenly reward is not predicated on belief in a supreme being, nor on ethical conduct, the by-product of religious faith. The individual can violate every religious tenet and still enter the euphoric kingdom. Thus the Near Death Experience offers secular man bargain basement salvation or, to use Bonhoeffer's phrase, "cheap grace." *The myth promises immortality and demands nothing in return.*

The myth meets our need for a supreme being who approves everything we do. Gone is the God of Scripture who calls men and women to account for sin and human folly. Because secular man believes he is essentially sinless or, at worst, "mistaken," he needs nothing more than a warm, cozy being of light to guide him on his way. Princeton theologian Daniel Migliore notes that Moody's deity has more in common with our notions of a good counselor than it does with the Holy One of Israel. Migliore writes:

> Does the "Being of Light" resemble, functionally speaking, a sympathetic therapist or sensitivity-group leader? Is the message that everything is OK, that even in our most selfish acts we were learning and growing, and that "self-realization" is the ultimate end of life really so unlike what we should have expected in a society saturated with cults of therapy and a philosophy of self-realization?[16]

Ludwig Feuerbach, a nineteenth century philosopher whose atheistic writings influenced both Freud and Marx, wrote that God is simply a projection of idealized human attributes. In other words, we create a being who embodies what we would like to be. I find it hard to believe man would construct a deity like the one we find in the Bible—a God who judges evil and continually calls man to repent. I find it easy to accept Feuerbach's thesis, however, when I see how easily the being of light fits into our anything-goes culture. Is this mysterious entity little more than our own projection of a nonjudgmental therapist?

Perhaps, too, in a deeper sense, the myth attracts because it fits our egocentric conception of history. For the past twenty years Americans have believed that they live in a golden age, a time that is special because they are special. Baby-boomers who became adults in the late sixties possessed more wealth, more free time, more opportunities for education and travel than any other generation. Mistaking economic and social privilege for innate superiority, they proclaimed the advent of the Aquarian age. Peace and love would abound, wars would cease, and a new world would emerge from their influence. The citizens of the new age rejected the past. If the individual and his society were unique, there seemed little sense in looking to history for answers. Although aspects of preindustrial society were romanticized, generally the past was discarded. This was especially true of traditional religion. The problem with the God of the Bible was that he was part of the old order. A deity who dealt with a primitive culture, so to speak, had little to say to a mature one. Christianity particularly came under attack because its central figure, Jesus of Nazareth, appeared two thousand years before the golden age began.

It was thought that if a messiah were to come, he would do so in the present enlightened era. Thus people joined cults in droves not only for the womb-like security they provided, but also to be near the charismatic leaders who fashioned these groups. The idea that "the messiah" lived among them confirmed their special place in history. I have seen this attitude, for example, among members of the Unification Church. There is a sense of excitement in being one of the "chosen ones," historically, who live during the same period as the "Lord of the Second Advent," Sun Myung Moon.

Our need to find new gods is also reflected in popular movies and books. The film that inaugurated the era in the late sixties was Stanley Kubrick's *2001: A Space Odyssey*. In that movie we pondered a rectangular monolith that appears to spacemen on the moon and then draws them to Jupiter and beyond. After seeing *2001*, a friend said that he had finally found "God." Many shared his view. Kubrick's effort spawned imitators. *Close Encounters of the Third Kind* depicts man's encounter with aliens as a religious experience of sight and sound. *Star Wars* introduced us to "The Force," an inscrutable presence that controls the universe and works for its salvation through the effort of Luke Skywalker. Even a "schlockbuster" like *Superman* has religious overtones. As the infant Superman hurtles toward earth in a space capsule, his "heavenly father," Jor-El, intones that his son will save mankind. As an adult, the Man of Steel proceeds to do so, especially at the end of the movie, when he resurrects Lois Lane.

Along with films there were books that satisfied our hunger for new deities. Erik von Daniken's best seller, *Chariots of the Gods*, started the movement. Von Daniken and subsequent writers theorized that certain archaeological finds indicated that our planet had been visited by "gods" from other worlds. In primeval times these aliens planted seeds from which ancient civilizations grew. Thus man's universal idea of a god in the heavens stems from a faint reminiscence.

Moody's being of light fits neatly into the cultural

context. The being may have been there throughout history, but he is eminently ours, since we only discovered him scientifically in 1975. We proved what previous generations only perceived dimly. Thus like the terrestrial gods of the cults and the celestial beings of books and movies, the being of light reinforces our own sense of historical egotism.

Four decades before the birth of Christ the Roman poet Virgil anticipated the future when he wrote:

> The final age now has come foretold in Cumae's song;
> The great sequence of centuries is being born anew.
> Now returns the Virgin, returns Saturn's reign,
> Now a new generation from high heaven sent...
> Dear offspring of the gods, Jove's great
>   augmenting seed![17]

Virgil wrote about the birth of the Augustan age, but his poetry applies equally to our era. We believe we are the offspring of the gods, and we have the deities in all shapes and forms to prove it. Commenting on our need to create new deities, social critic Tom Wolfe writes: "God is dead and forty new gods live, prancing like mummers."[18]

In viewing ourselves through the prism of earlier Christian cultures, we can see how unique we are. In the past, Christian Everyman believed one worked to attain salvation. There were theologians like Augustine and Luther to remind him that he was saved by faith in Jesus Christ rather than by good deeds. Nevertheless Everyman understood that one could not receive heavenly reward by ignoring or actively opposing biblical injunctions. There was a connection between this life and the next. He realized, too, that God was a righteous judge as well as a loving father, and that judgment and love were united in the godhead for his salvation. In other words, Everyman was cognizant of sin. Finally, even if he lived during a prosperous age, he never thought enlightened culture had outgrown its need for the Holy One of the Old and New Testaments. Finding parallels between his world and biblical culture, he believed God was sufficient for all times and places.

Biblical Considerations

The Bible gives little support to the Near Death Experience. Moody argues that Stephen's execution in the book of Acts illustrates his findings. Before he is stoned by the Jerusalem authorities, the first Christian martyr sees "the glory of God, and Jesus standing at the right hand of God" (Acts 7:55). This is simply a vision rather than a discarnate journey toward future life. Stephen's spirit does not leave his body nor, for that matter, is he even dying when he sees God's splendor. He has not reached his execution site.

Moody's findings have more affinity with Greek religion than biblical faith. There are biblical accounts of souls departing bodies, but these are few and far between. They do not give information about the life to come, nor do they indicate that the out-of-body experience is normative for the living or dying. Unlike Greek religion, the Bible stresses the unity of the individual—mind, soul, and body—under the Lordship of God. Discarnate entities floating above bodies and spiritual junkets to the world beyond are foreign to its theological landscape.

Essentially the Near Death Experience fails in the crisis of dying because humans yearn for more than survival after death. Man is programmed to believe that eternity is wrapped up in Jesus Christ. We long to know the Son of God, the One who has always known and loved us. Thus even if science could show that the Hotel Bliss awaited us, death would be terrifying still. Brushes with terminality, as Ted's case illustrates, convince us that heavenly mansions, angels on clouds, and the being of light, our own projections of ourselves, are all of no account. In fact, without the presence of Jesus Christ at its core, afterlife is only as hopeful as nonexistence. This is why the Bible speaks of eternal life rather than immortality. The latter is not relational; it signifies only that our spirit goes on after death. The concept of eternal life brings immortality into present history, in a sense. We can only understand and desire future life when we accept Jesus Christ in the here and now. In our daily lives together, Jesus assures us, as he did his first disciples, that fellowship with him will continue, that immortality will have content.

> Let not your heart be troubled; you believe in God, believe also in Me. In My Father's house are many mansions; if it were not so, I would have told you. I go to prepare a place for you. And if I go and prepare a place for you, I will come again and receive you to Myself; that where I am, there you may be also (John 14:1–3).

Our Lord doesn't dwell on the nature of afterlife; he simply assures us that the relationship we have in the present will continue.

Jesus' resurrection also points to eternal life rather than immortality. It is not simply that he emerged from the tomb to show us that we, too, would rise after death. More fully we understand with whom we shall share our resurrected states. When we examine the Gospels, we are struck by the similarity between Jesus' postresurrection appearances and his life before the crucifixion. Once again Jesus encounters fishermen casting their nets on the Sea of Galilee. He inquires about their work and invites them to breakfast. Once again he walks with them on a dusty road outside Jerusalem, listening to their sorrow, sharing their humanity. Later that day he enters their home and breaks bread at supper. Perhaps, in the single most poignant scene in the resurrection narratives, Jesus encounters the woman from whom he cast out seven demons, as she weeps near his tomb. He restores their friendship simply by saying her name, "Mary," the way, we imagine, he spoke to her so many times in the past.

We might have expected spiritual pyrotechnics when the Son of Man rose from the dead. We don't get them. Jesus doesn't whisk his followers away on a cloud and regale them with descriptions of dying experiences or accounts of immortality. Once again he simply abides with them during the day. By focusing on a return to daily fellowship, Jesus minimizes the finality of death and emphasizes the continuity between what is and what is to come. The resurrection narratives assure the believer that present life with Christ is similar to future life.

It is not immortality that frees us from fear of death, but rather belief in eternal life, a process that begins in history. Present fellowship with Christ prepares us to die in two ways. First, when we accept him as Lord, we begin to see that crucifixion and resurrection, far from being singular events, are recurrent themes in our lives. Throughout our personal journeys, we suffer "crucifixions." We may experience unemployment, poverty, divorce, sickness, grief, bouts of depression, any number of terrible happenings. In minor as well as major events, we often feel as if the bottom has dropped out of our lives. I know people who have felt like "doing themselves in" for losing house keys or wallets. As Christians, however, we begin to understand that Jesus transforms tragedy into new life for us. Again and again. In other words, we experience a metaphoric resurrection as we walk in faith. This is the pattern we carry when we enter the hospital for the last time. Although dying is the biggest hurdle man must face, Christians believe their savior will transform this great negative into new life because they have seen Christ's resurrecting power in the past. Thus death is relativized. We view it as another crucifixion event along the road of eternal life.

Our present day relationship with Jesus Christ prepares us for terminality in another respect. Faith teaches us to die to self. As we grow in Christ, we learn to surrender who we are and what we want for the sake of the gospel. Jesus said that whoever "loses his life for My sake will find it"(Matt. 10:39), and we find this is eminently true. Surrendering self and trusting in Christ bring life in abundance. Thus we take this pattern of living into the dying experience. Because we have died to ourselves figuratively in the past, it becomes easier to die literally in the present. We have learned good will comes whenever we surrender our lives to our Lord.

The message of the New Testament is that we die the way we live. If we place our hope in the concept of immortality, we arm ourselves with false security. As we die, our instinct desires a person, not a blissful state or heavenly place. If we have known Christ in this life, we will be able to discern his face in the face of death. The French theologian Pierre Teilhard de Chardin puts it well when he writes:

At that moment when I feel I am losing hold of myself and am absolutely passive within the hands of the great unknown forces that have formed me...O, God, grant that I may understand that it is You (provided only that my faith is strong enough) who are painfully parting the fibres of my being in order to penetrate to the very marrow of my substance and bear me away within Yourself.[19]

6

The Myth of Mind over Death

"Mind over Death" is the first minor myth we shall examine. It presents the idea that science has shown us how to overcome terminality by unlocking the power of the mind. We can prevent or cure terminal illness by assuming an optimistic stance. Unlike the major myths, Mind over Death treats mortality as an enemy rather than a friend. However, it disguises the nature of death by saying that it is easily solved. We get the impression that the Grim Reaper can be forestalled indefinitely by the power of positive thinking.

Psychotherapist Lawrence LeShan is perhaps the foremost exponent of the mind-over-death mentality. Before we examine the main points of his best seller, I must say something about the particular disease from which his findings are derived. Cancer is the malady that more than any other signifies death in the twentieth century. Writing in 1928 George Groddeck, one of the most influential psychiatrists of his day, noted: "Of all the theories put forward in connection with cancer, only one in my opinion survived the passage of time, namely, that cancer leads through definite stages to death. I mean by that that what is not fatal is not cancer."[1] I have seen the truth of Groddeck's statement in the lives of many families. When someone confesses the nature of his illness to loved ones, they secretly begin to plan his funeral. Recently I asked the seven-year-old daughter of a sick friend what the word *cancer* meant to her. She said it reminded her of "the place where people are buried."

We might think cancer connotes death because of mortality rates. According to the National Center for Health Statistics (Dec., 1984),[2] 433,795 people died from various forms of cancer in 1982. In other words, 1219 individuals died daily, nearly one a minute. The National Cancer Society estimates that three out of four families will be affected by the disease.[3] Although these statistics are frightening, they do not tell the whole story, since coronary disease is the number one killer in the country. In 1982, 755,592 people died of heart ailments, nearly twice the number of cancer victims. Yet heart disease simply does not inspire the dread cancer does.

I think there are several reasons why death and cancer have become synonymous. First, cancer is more mysterious than most diseases. Medical researchers are unsure what causes certain malignancies. Do hereditary considerations, viruses, or industrial pollutants trigger unnatural cell division? Or is it a combination of factors? Although scientists have discovered the cause of some cancers, others remain a mystery. The disease is also baffling because there is no single cure. The medical community cannot immunize a nation against cancer the way it did against polio. Instead of a cure-all vaccine, cancer treatment is viewed by the layman as a potpourri of tactics, many of which are ineffective. Finally, cancer is mysterious because it travels from one area to another. There is little mystery, in this respect, to heart disease. We know which organ it affects. But cancer has no exclusive domain. Often a secondary growth strays far from the primary tumor.

Cancer also frightens us because we associate it with intractable pain. Certainly not all cases are painful. Nevertheless, we have all heard or read about patients who needed morphine to relieve their agony. Our views are also shaped by personal experience. Many of us have sat at bedside and witnessed the teeth-clenched struggle of a loved one or friend. We have prayed that death might accomplish what the strongest narcotic could not. Not only do we associate physical distress with cancer itself, we also believe pain accompanies treatment. Many of us know someone who has endured the side effects of chemotherapy or radiation. Last year I returned to a former parish and visited Jacqueline, a sixteen-year-old member. Cured of a deadly lymphoma, she told me that the disease was not as painful as the bone marrow biopsy she underwent at the beginning of treatment.

Cancer frightens us for a third reason. The illness connotes physical deterioration. Most cancer patients I have known suffer an alarming loss of appetite. In spite of coaxing from friends and family, they will rarely eat what is set before them. Their weight plummets and their faces assume the gaunt, hollow-cheeked appearance we associate with the disease. When we think of emaciation, we think of cancer. This is especially frightening to a society that places great emphasis on physical appearance.

Finally, our fear of cancer has to do with the broad use of the word in our culture. Today cancer is not simply a name for an illness, but rather a metaphor for a host of social ills. The politician refers to inflation as a *cancerous* situation. Ministers describe sexual permissiveness or drug abuse as a *cancer* on the moral fiber of society. The social worker states that poverty is a fast growing *malignancy* within his community. Thus the word fills us with dread because it signifies evil in all of its forms.

For these, and perhaps other reasons, we equate cancer with death. Thus LeShan's book, *You Can Fight for Your Life: Emotional Factors in the Treatment of Cancer,* was greeted with acclaim because it seemingly attacked death *per se.* People perceived his theory as an answer to mortality and compared it to medical measures like radiation and chemotheraphy. The solution seemed relatively easy: Change your emotional patterns. LeShan, an experimental pyschologist who was working at the time out of the Institute of Applied Biology in New York City, conducted psychotherapies on seventy patients with terminal malignancies and psychological profiles on other chronically ill patients. He notes that people are cancer prone because of their personality. The disease is brought on by a psychological orientation that first allows malignant cells to invade and then represses the individual's disease coping mechanisms.

The typical cancer personality, says LeShan, manifests a number of emotional traits. First he cannot accept the loss of a central relationship. He becomes emotionally directionless when a loved one is removed from his life. The problem, which usually involves the death of a spouse or parent, need not be recent. According to LeShan, unresolved grief in childhood can lead to cancer in adulthood. Second, the typical cancer victim cannot express resentment. He may get angry at another's plight, but never at his own. LeShan cites several cases in which individuals were living in the manner prescribed by their parents. Instead of lashing out at their families, they suppressed their anger, which eventually manifested itself in cancer. Third, the cancer prone individual is filled with self-contempt. According to LeShan, his patients perceived themselves as stupid, lazy, or mediocre—assessments that had little basis in reality. Although many were successful, they could not accept accolades from others because of their deep-rooted sense of inferiority. Fourth, the individual's life is marked by despair. He does not believe he will ever achieve meaning or satisfaction in this life. Rather, fate has conspired against him. Cancer is a sign that life has dealt him a losing hand. If the individual displays one or more of these characteristics, LeShan believes he should change his lifestyle or consult a cancer specialist.

Although the psychotherapist qualifies himself by noting other causes and cures of cancer, the reader easily infers that the mind is either the sole culprit or the sole savior. The most impressive part of the book is the healings effected by counseling. LeShan notes that his method helps the patient focus on what is right with him, rather than a more traditional approach which explores the individual's weaknesses. If the terminally ill patient can feel good about himself and live fully without restraint from others, cancer is likely to leave his system. LeShan's clients usually end up changing careers or spouses on the way to physical health.

Though popular, LeShan's theories are not new. During the eighteenth and nineteenth centuries particularly, a number of physicians were saying much the same. In 1783 a physician wrote: "A cancer is caused by the uneasy passions of the mind with which a patient is affected for a long time that weaken the circulations of the blood and thicken it."[4] In 1871 one G. Von Schmitt, a physician who treated the writer Alexandre Dumas for a malignancy, listed "deep and sedentary study and pursuits, the feverish and anxious agitation of public life, the cares of ambition, frequent paroxysms of rage, violent grief"[5] as primary causes of cancer. Changing one's emotional outlook was offered as a cure to the terminally ill patient. One doctor noted that if one practiced "perseverance, pluck, and determination" for a period of "one to four years,"[6] the cancer would vanish. A few physicians even warned individuals to avoid vocations that could produce a negative frame of mind. In 1846 Walter Hayle Walsh, an English surgeon and professor, wrote:

> The ordinary considerations in respect of general healthfulness, which serve to guide parents in the selection of a profession for their sons, should have their due weight in cancerous families. But there is one circumstance to be especially borne in mind, and of more importance than all others in such families—I mean the avoidance of a profession the active and serious exercise of which entails more or less constant care and anxiety. The importance of this consideration appears from what I have said on the influence of mental suffering in generating the disease. For this reason, the professions of the Bar, Medicine, and Diplomacy should be avoided. The speculations in which merchants, bankers, stockbrokers, etc., are so prone to indulge, ought, if these occupations be embraced, to be systematically shunned for the same obvious motives. All things considered, the professions of the Army, Navy and the Church, unless there be some special objection, offer the best chances of escape from the diseases to individuals predisposed to cancer. Females should not become governesses.[7]

The emotional causation of cancer was given impetus

during this period due to the cultural view of women. Considered the weaker sex, it was assumed that females had far more trouble handling their emotions than men. Throughout the literature of this period, words like *hysteria*, and phrases like "passions of the mind" are associated with women. It was easy, then, to link emotions with cancer because the disease was thought to afflict females far more than males. In 1759 the physician Richard Guy wrote that "women are more subject to Cancerous Disorders than Men, especially such Women as are of sedentary, melancholic Disposition of Mind, and meet with such Disasters in Life, as occasion much trouble and Grief."[8] Like other physicians of the day, Guy based his conclusions on the high incidence of breast cancer. Because many malignancies were either unknown or mistaken for other illnesses, it was assumed that cancer of the breast was the primary form of the disease. Thus "female emotions" were linked to a "female malady."

Far from being unique to cancer alone, however, psychological causation has always been attractive to cultures faced with diseases of epidemic proportion, diseases which refuse to submit to science of the day. During the 1300s, when bubonic plague decimated a third of European population, physicians were advising people to avoid anger before going to bed. In rat-infested London of the sixteenth century, it was commonly held that cheerful people were immune to the plague. Before a cure of tuberculosis was discovered, people in the nineteenth century believed the disease would not strike them as long as they smiled and avoided the melancholic artistic temperament of the time.

LeShan's theory has been popular throughout history, whenever man faced a terrifying killer he could not understand. Indeed, the idea of psychological causation was more popular among scientists in earlier cultures than it is now. In 1621 Robert Burton summarized much of what civilization knew about illness. Disease, the reader is told, is caused by an imbalance of bodily humors, evil spirits, and unhealthy foods, like bread made from oats. Burton also notes:

> For as the body works upon the mind by his bad humors, troubling the spirits, sending gross fumes into the brain, and so per consequence disturbing the soul, and all the faculties of it...So on the other side, the mind most effectively works upon the body, producing by his passions and perturbations miraculous alterations, as melancholy, despair, cruel diseases and sometimes death itself.[9]

Scientific Problems

Although it acquired some scientific support in the past, does the myth of Mind over Death meet empirical criteria today? While many researchers acknowledge the part emotions play in any illness, they do not say one's psyche is the primary cause of cancer. Dr. Jimmie C. Holand, Chief of Psychiatry Service at Memorial Sloan-Kettering Cancer Center in New York, writes: "There is no evidence in human beings that persons who are under high levels of stress by occupation or life-style are more apt to develop cancer."[10] Yet he notes that stress reaction may produce change in endocrine and immunological systems in the body, which may have a bearing on cancer. Edward J. Beatti, another researcher at Sloan-Kettering, notes that "a positive outlook aids recovery," but he warns against elevating a positive frame of mind as an alternative cancer treatment.[11] Important studies in the area of breast and cervical cancers indicate there is little correlation between cancer and personality.[12]

There are also specific problems with research in this area. Much of it is anecdotal. Dr. Theodore Miller, a defender of psychological causation, admitted to a group of fellow cancer specialists that scientific studies had proved little; therefore his lecture would be limited to a few case histories from his file.[13] Even work buttressed by statistics has come under fire from Dr. Bernard Fox of the field studies and statistics program at the National Cancer Institute. Dr. Fox notes that most studies dealing with the cancer personality are rife with statistical and sampling errors. There is no way we can identify a cancer personality, Dr. Fox believes, from the data we are given.[14]

Another problem with research in this area is that most studies compare people who already have cancer to those who do not. This is the weakness in LeShan's study. Compared to healthy people, cancer patients suffer more from feelings of anger, despair, and helplessness. It is likely, however, that negative feelings are offshoots of the disease rather than causative agents. Dr. Irving Cramer, founder of the Oneida County Tumor Clinic (N. Y.), told me that patients who seem emotionally healthy before cancer often undergo drastic transformation after the onset of the disease. Dr. Cramer attributed this to biological changes brought on by the illness and attitudinal shifts of family and friends toward the cancer patient.[15] In an important study, Finn, Mulcahy, and Hickey concluded that the overriding anxiety of the cancer patient makes it impossible to assess the individual's personality prior to cancer.[16] Dr. P. B.

Medawar, a tumor specialist and Nobel Prize winner, noted that even if psychic negativity characterizes the individual before illness, this, too, may be the product of cancer rather than personality, since malignancies can lie dormant in the human system for as long as fifty years without surfacing.[17]

The fundamental problem with LeShan's study is that the "cancer personality," as he describes it, is too general. It fits nearly everyone. At some time in their lives, most people have trouble coping with the loss of a central relationship. Most people, too, repress anger and feel inferior. Haven't many of us gone through periods when life itself seemed to conspire against us? Rather than a personality type prone to illness, LeShan has described the human condition.

Practical Problems

The myth of Mind over Death is practically dangerous as well as theoretically suspect. Patients who believe the mind is the preventive or cure factor of disease set themselves up for trouble, as the following cases illustrate.

Larry

Larry had twenty-three radiation treatments in two months. The x-rays had reduced the growth in his lung but also weakened him sufficiently to warrant hospitalization. One evening I played priest and listened to his confession. Angry at himself instead of God, Larry viewed his illness as the product of a character flaw. Larry's father died when he was a little boy. An only child, he had taken care of his mother most of his life. At the time of her death, Larry's hardware store verged on bankruptcy due to the financial mismanagement of an accountant. The combination put him in the hospital where he gradually eased out of his depression. Several months after hospitalization, he met and married Margaret. She helped him manage the store and, for eight years, his life went smoothly. When I visited the hospital, Larry's optimism had vanished. He was troubled by his past as well as his disease. "If my mind had been stronger, if I hadn't fallen apart," he said, "I'd be fine today."

The myth of Mind over Death saddled Larry with guilt and despair. He condemned himself for not preventing his cancer. I have known others who have damned themselves for not curing theirs. If the vaccine or antidote to a life-threatening illness is embedded in one's mind then, logically, the disease signals a defect in personality. Cancer becomes a tangible sign of weak will or character flaw. The prevalence of this myth accounts for changes in attitude toward the cancer patient. Instead of a sick individual, society often sees an emotional outcast, someone who has failed himself and others. Often it is the fear of moral rather than physical contagion that keeps people away from the bedside.

Gail

Gail's case illustrates the major problem with the myth under consideration. An attractive twenty-four year old, Gail had just completed an M.A. in English literature when I visited her in the hospital. Highly motivated, she excelled in everything she tried. She was given major parts in dramatic productions and held her college's high jump record. We talked the night before her mastectomy. Scared by its implication, she had waited a couple of months before telling anyone about the lump in her breast. A part of her admitted, however, that if it were cancer, she could cure it herself. A reader of Far Eastern philosophy, Gail focused her mind's eye, as she put it, on the cyst. Unfortunately, it continued to grow. When the swelling became painful, she informed her parents and called a doctor. After surgery, at the beginning of her hospital stay, she noted that dying was a natural event, and nothing to fear. Gail could voice this opinion, I believe, because she thought her positive attitude in the past would allow her to survive. For added insurance, she surrounded herself with positive thinking manuals and even a book on assertiveness training. The more she realized massive doses of optimism would not alter the course of her illness, the more frightened she became. Believing she could avoid death, she was unprepared to deal with a reality that smashed her psychological amulets with impunity.

The myth of Mind over Death also complicates the lives of loved ones who stand at bedside, as the following cases illustrate.

Ralph

Ralph's wife, Mary, lost the desire to work when cutbacks in state aid crippled the hospital department she had spent twenty-three years of her life building. After quitting, she flung herself into church activities and fund raising jobs for the community chest. She hoped volunteer work would fill her emptiness. It didn't. About a year after she left her nursing position, Mary discovered she had lung cancer. Six months after the diagnosis she died. Ralph blamed himself for her demise because he thought greater understanding on his part during her emotional upheaval would have prevented cancer cells from invading. Although Ralph was a model husband, he had trouble forgiving himself for his perceived neglect. Thus the myth added guilt to his grief.

Marion

Both Marion and Sol believed the mind could cure all things, a faith that sustained them until Sol contracted cancer. In the hospital they presented a united front, practicing meditation, biofeedback, and other holistic healing methods. Marion began distancing herself from Sol, however, as his disease progressed. She would arrive late for visits and, on a few occasions, did not appear. She came for help when she could no longer rationalize her behavior. As she spoke, we both sensed the extent of her anger. Finally she screamed, "Why doesn't he help himself? Why is he doing this?" I told Marion that anger is a natural response to the imminent loss of a spouse.

The question that is often thought but rarely voiced is: "How can he leave when I need him?" The grieving person soon realizes that anger, though understandable, is unjustified. The terminally ill patient did not choose his malady. Nearly all would rather live than die. The myth, however, provides a rationale for anger as Marion's case illustrates. The impression is that the individual chose not to heal himself, thereby scarring loved ones. Listening to Marion, I got the impression Sol brought on his cancer to spite her. Another woman whose husband died of multiple sclerosis said much the same thing. Her husband hadn't loved her or himself sufficiently to get well. Thus Mind over Death drives a wedge between the patient and his spouse, at a time when he needs a loved one's support the most.

Why We Believe

Although the myth causes problems for the dying and their families, it serves as a palliative for the healthy. The answer to sickness and death is simple: If one cultivates a positive frame of mind, renegade cells will never coalesce. The optimistic individual need not worry about cancer, or the common cold for that matter. The myth of Mind over Death fits neatly into a society hooked on easy solutions. Not long ago a friend from England remarked, "You Americans find answers as easily as a magician pulls rabbits out of a hat." Coming from a country that has yet to solve the problem of central heating gives him, he believes, ability to cope with difficulties of long standing. Many Americans have lost this capacity. In the past twenty years we have embraced therapies and religions that promise to transform our lives—in the course of a weekend. Instead of struggling with existence, we by-pass it by taking drugs of all kinds. Our cultural storehouse is stocked with volumes explaining how to build muscles, lose weight, gain confidence, write novels, and paint like Picasso in "five easy steps" or "two short weeks." Our intellectual warehouse, the university, coddles students. We substitute courses that explore the content of comics for rigorous curricula. According to the columnist George Will, it is possible to get a baccalaureate degree from an Ivy League institution without reading the classics or struggling with great ideas of the past.

In the marketplace, too, hard work is devalued, as any number of lazy man's guides to success indicate. In *Winning Through Intimidation,* one of the most popular books of this genre, Robert Ringer notes: "Reality is such that it simply isn't true that if you do a good job, you'll get what you deserve. That kind of attitude will turn you into a cob-web covered skeleton with a pile of cigar butts where your chips should be."[18] Advocating the easy road, Ringer substitutes manipulation for persistence and hard work. Problems are solved easily, we are told, if you know the right psychological buttons to push.

Sixty second solutions are found in the relationships market as well. Self-help manuals tell us that one need only follow a simple, step-by-step method to a happy marriage—or creative divorce. Advertising's message is even simpler. Selection of the right soap, cologne, or mouthwash is all the individual needs for success with the opposite sex. Indeed, our tendency is to jettison relationships that require more effort than our self-help tomes and commercials suggest. We live at a time when a goal's worth is measured by the ease it takes to attain it. In such a society, the idea that one can smile death away is appealing.

The second reason the myth attracts is that it provides society with criteria for scapegoating. In other words, Mind over Death defines who will succumb to terminal illness. Throughout history, cultures have dealt with their fear of killer diseases by making scapegoats of individuals or groups. Scapegoating offers the illusion of safety by removing illness from the general social context. It is not the population at large, but only a small subsection that is disease prone, we believe. Finding a whipping boy also allows society to vent its rage against illness and death. Be it plague or cancer, humans need to punish a portion of the community for maladies they cannot understand or control. We see this behavior in medieval Europe, for example, where Jews and gypsies were routinely executed as plague carriers. In Puritan

New England, witch hunts went hand in hand with epidemics.

Today we punish the individual with cancer particularly, although our method of dealing with the scapegoat is subtler than cultural practices of the past. We limit him vocationally. Society has done much to ameliorate gender, race, and age discrimination in the marketplace, yet cancer patients are still denied work or advancement because of their illness. A friend could not understand why his progress up the corporate ladder was blocked, until an associate pulled out his résumé. The word *cancer* had been underlined in red ink. My friend had contracted skin cancer twenty years earlier as a teen-ager. There had been no recurrence of the disease. I have known others who lied on job applications because they knew that even mentioning that they had been cured could be the vocational kiss of death.

Commenting on society's punitive tendency in the job market, social philospher Susan Sontag writes that those who have or have had cancer tend to be "extremely prudish, if not outright secretive about their disease."[19] The extent of the problem is reflected in the Freedom of Information Act of 1966. Cancer is the only disease whose disclosure is thought to be an unwarranted invasion of privacy. In formulating the law, Congress realized the power of cancer to stigmatize vocationally. By helping society define the problem, the myth of Mind over Death aids in the persecution of those "tainted" by life-threatening illness.

Perhaps the most important reason the myth attracts is that it stresses individuality. We need no one but ourselves to master disease and forestall death. Family, medical personnel, hospitals are only peripheral factors in the struggle against serious illness. These ideas are very popular in a culture that marks a person's success by the ability to "go it alone." In a deeper sense, Mind over Death fits our particular brand of American individualism. In its native form, the individual fulfills himself by forgetting or rejecting others. In 1835 the French observer Alexis de Tocqueville noted that Americans' pioneering spirit went hand in hand with their detachment from community. "The woof of time is every instant broken and the track of generations effaced," de Tocqueville wrote. "Those who went before are soon forgotten; of those who will come after, no one has any idea; the interest of man is confined to those in close propinquity to himself."[20]

Nearly 150 years later, social critic Peter Marin noted that our tendency to reject significant others on our way to self-understanding had become worse than preceding generations. In order to be "self-actualized," Americans turned their backs on the basic social unit, the family. Mother, father, spouse, child were all though to be inimical to one's psychic health.[21] One had to free himself from the constraints of those closest to him. The myth fits the cultural pattern for it assumes the patient must remove the ties of family if he is to be healed. Taking a psychoanalytic approach, LeShan notes that the cancer personality is formed by problems within the family. The emotional instability of the cancer patient is the result of Father's rejection of Mother, or vice versa. His chronic depression is the product of conflict with unrealistic parental expectations early on in life. The cure, for LeShan, is the American brand of individualism on a medical plane. One can save his life from cancer or other dread diseases simply by rejecting filial influence and becoming his own person.

When we look at Christian Everyman, we realize how

different he is from secular representatives of our culture. Unlike his modern counterpart, Everyman realized life was a struggle. Problems were rarely solved at the drop of a hat. Indeed he often viewed earthly vicissitudes as mysteries that could not be fully understood until he reached heaven. This was especially true of terminal illness. He also understood that the enigmatic nature of life was, in a sense, a blessing. It demanded he put his faith in God.

Everyman did not believe he could engineer his own salvation when it came to death. At God's appointed time, disease would take him, whether or not he thought positive thoughts. Epidemics made Everyman especially aware of his finite nature. He looked to God rather than self for healing. More than his modern counterpart, he also looked to others for support. Eschewing the idea of individualism, he called on the church, as well as his family, as he lay dying. If a healing miracle took place, he thanked God—and the community of believers who made intercession on his behalf. If there was no miracle, Everyman gleaned hope from ecclesiastical representatives at his bedside. The idea of Mind over Death was foreign to him.

Biblical Considerations

In the Bible man never forestalls or conquers death by the power of his mind. Our dying, as well as our living, is contingent on the will of God alone. In Deuteronomy, God states: "Now see that I, even I, am He, and there is no God besides Me; I kill and make alive; I wound and I heal; nor is there any who can deliver from My hands" (32:39). Thus whether man changes his personality or stands on his head matters little in the final outcome. We die when God ordains it.

It is interesting to note that biblical characters often live to ripe ages, even when their emotional outlook might be considered less than satisfactory by today's psychotherapeutic standards. Moses is a good example. He seems to be a prime candidate for early cancer, yet he lived to be 120. Moses suffered from low self-esteem. He did not think he was capable of doing what the Lord requested. There were others, he felt, who were better fitted for the task. It is easy to infer he had trouble early with his family. His natural mother was forced to abandon him when he was infant. Perhaps, too, strife with his adoptive Egyptian family occurred when Moses began to understand his Jewish identity. At times he must have felt as if life had dealt him a losing hand. Going against Pharaoh day after day was emotionally draining. He took a psychic battering after the Exodus, when his own people blamed him for their new-found problems with freedom.

By LeShan's standards, Moses suffered enough emotional trauma to kill an army. Yet, as the great leader's case illustrates, God upholds his own whether or not they are models of mental health. Let me say that by today's standards many were not. Serving God often meant undergoing psychic stress of the first order. Jeremiah, for example, complained bitterly about his role as prophet and, at one point, contemplated suicide. Nevertheless, if his forty-year ministry is any indication, he did not die prematurely from cancer. Implicit in the Bible is the idea that we are maintained by God's love rather than our own efforts to protect or save ourselves.

The fact that God is sovereign over death is not a call for passivity or resignation in the face of life-threatening illness. We are not to surrender psychologically, for until death arrives, we don't know what God's will for us is. He may want us to receive a miracle and be physically healed. Or he may want us to die and come fully into his presence. Because we cannot second-guess the Almighty, our task is to look to him for salvation and fight sickness with the mental resources he has given us. Many of Jesus' miracles were cooperative affairs. The patient used willpower to appropriate Christ's healing. Thus although Jesus annointed the eyes of the blind man, healing became a reality only when he washed in the pool of Siloam as the Lord directed (see John 9:1–11). The paralytic was cured only when he picked up his bed and walked (see Matt. 9:1–7). There is no indication Jesus took him by the hand and helped him to his feet. In several cases, healing occurred after the individual admitted his desire to get well. In other words, a hopeful stance was a prerequisite for Jesus' action. Thus in the Gospels we often see that a patient's mind worked in conjunction with Christ for the cure. A positive attitude is important, but—and this is the crucial point—it is never a substitute for God. The deification of the mind has no place in the Bible. This is certainly made clear in Jesus' greatest miracle, the resurrection of Lazarus (see John 11:1–44). At the tomb in Bethany, we are aware of God's raw power to cure, unconditioned by man's thinking.

Let me add, too, that Jesus heals whether or not we are cured of serious illness. Certainly the individual who is healed miraculously has a message of hope to share with others. But so also does the believer who is not cured. Often I have seen great miracles in the lives of those who have but a few weeks to live. There is a transformation of the spirit, if not the body, that convicts the world of the healing power of Jesus Christ.

John is a good example. At age eighteen, he was dying of leukemia. Although he had always been a Christian, suddenly, during the last period of his life, he was touched by the hand of God. He started praying with other patients and doing odds and ends like fluffing pillows of the bedridden. One day I saw him strolling down the corridor with a little boy. The child was attatched to a portable I.V. bottle, and John read a story as they walked hand in hand. I believe John compressed more meaning and fulfillment in three or four short weeks than in eighteen years of living.

To say God is sovereign over death gives us the freedom to live fully in the present. We can risk for the sake of the gospel, knowing he will take care of our ultimate future. Belief in the myth, on the other hand, robs us of life because we spend more time analyzing than living. If we alone control our ultimate destiny, we must be eternally vigilant. We ask, have we done enough to change the psychic effect of a negative childhood, or a traumatic incident in adolescence? Have we freed ourselves from depression and repressed anger? Are we viewing the future with sufficient optimism? For the devotee of Mind over Death, life becomes a psychic mine field filled with cancer causing explosives, ready to detonate if he fails to tread lightly. He cannot embrace life spontaneously, the way Jesus did, because he is too busy protecting himself.

To say God is in control of our death also frees us from the need to blame ourselves or others for terminal illness. We may question why God allows us to die at a particular point in our lives. What purpose does it serve, when we have children to raise and goals to accomplish? With faith, however, we realize answers will be forthcoming in the next life. There is no such assurance for the believer in Mind over Death since he thinks he alone is responsible for his dying. Abrogating the position of

God, he has no recourse but to pray to himself.

The myth under consideration *increases our fear of death*. Because the believer cannot leave death to God, it intrudes into the everyday. The subject becomes a factor in decisions he makes and crises he undergoes. It is only in handing to God what we cannot order or control that we find ourselves opening to possibilities of abundant life.

CHAPTER
7

The Myth of
Medical Immortality

The final myth we shall examine is that of "Medical Immortality." Of the four, it goes furthest in stressing the omnipotence of science. The idea is that man can forestall or possibly eliminate death in the near future due to advances in technology. Thus if one takes care of himself until the great medical breakthrough, he may live longer than Methuselah. The book we shall examine is Albert Rosenfeld's *Prolongevity*, the most popular treatment of the topic in the seventies. Unlike other authors I have discussed, Rosenfeld compiles the research of others rather than positing his own theory. He focuses primarily on genetic and endocrinological hypotheses of aging. In the first area, Rosenfeld details the research of men like Leonard Hayflick of Stanford, who believes the clock of aging, as he puts it, is found in the cell. DNA, the basic molecule of life, which is part of each cell's nucleus, monitors the cell's activity and at some point tells it to slow down. Although some researchers believe that cells in cultures can live forever, Hayflick's experiments show that each cell has a limited lifespan which, he believes, is dictated by the DNA, or genetic code in the nucleus. In other words, each cell carries the seeds of its own destruction. Thus, at some point specialized cells in our body die. Many more cells, however, lose their capacity to reproduce by dividing. Over a gradual period of time the individual's cellular structure changes, he grows old, and dies.

The other major theory that Rosenfeld explores is aging and death via the endocrine system. The endocrine system is composed of glands in the body that regulate its function. Rosenfeld explores the work of W. Donner Denckla, a researcher from the Roche Institute of Molecular Biology, who believes the pituitary gland in the brain secretes a death hormone that affects cell function. This hormone, which Denckla calls DECO (decreasing oxygen consumption), may prevent cells from utilizing oxygen by suppressing the effect of another hormone, thyroxin. Thus the cell slowly dies.

Along with the work of Hayflick and Denckla, Rosenfeld also discusses other hopeful areas in longevity research. He notes positive results in hypothermia experiments. Some studies have shown that lowering body temperature in certain animals increases lifespan. Other studies have shown that restricting diet in animals, especially when they are young, retards the aging process.

Interesting work has also been done in the area of parabiosis, the transfusion of two organisms. The blood of a young rat, introduced into the system of an older one, often produces rejuvenation. In one study, the cholesterol levels of older rats went down "almost miraculously" after transfusion. In another study, the parabiotic union between young and old cockroaches allowed the old ones to regenerate limbs, a capacity that a young roach alone possesses.

Rosenfeld even notes work done to increase longevity through the power of suggestion. Lawrence Casler, a psychologist at the State University of New York (Geneseo), has conducted experiments in which he tells hypnotized patients they will live to be 120. Casler, a firm believer in medical immortality, hopes to be around to assess the results of his study. Although many streams of research are moving in a positive direction, according to Rosenfeld, our greatest hope for increased lifespan comes from the research of men like Hayflick and Denckla. We must either understand, then dismantle the cellular clock of aging through genetic tampering, or isolate the death hormone, and then find a suitable antidote.

Rosenfeld believes a significant lengthening of the human lifespan will occur in the next few decades and that "by the year 2025—if the research proceeds at reasonable speed—most of the major mysteries of the aging process will have been solved, and the solutions adopted as part of conventional biomedical knowledge."[1] Although he never states that we are on the verge of man-made immortality, he implies it. To those who suggest that although science may improve the quality of our lifespan, it will neither lengthen it significantly nor abolish death, Rosenfeld waxes eloquently about how technology has bamboozled experts in the past:

> It is hard to think of anything that exists in our civilized lives that would not once have been declared impossible. Look at a jumbo jet, with 350 passengers aboard. See them lifted aloft and carried across the ocean in a few hours—carried in comfort, too, fed a sumptuous meal, shown a movie, given a choice of seven stereo listening channels. That bizarre, implausible kind of

occurrence does, as we know, happen routinely every day, many times a day, in many parts of the world, One would not have to go very far back in time to find the world's sanest, most knowing authorities, confronted with such a description, pronouncing the kind of technological—and social—capacity to be among the more preposterous and unattainable fantasies they had ever heard.[2]

In other words, Rosenfeld implies that to rule out man-made immortality is foolishness given our scientific track record. The reader also infers that eternal life is within his grasp if he stays healthy until the biomedical golden age arrives. The individual may have a chance of making it if he eats lightly, exercises, and avoids stress. Then, too, the idea of medical immortality is gleaned from the book's dust cover. We are told that the dream of a Fountain of Youth in our lifetime may not be fanciful. "For if aging becomes merely another curable disease, we will perhaps have found a solution to the problem of death itself." Even if Rosenfeld wrote a disclaimer on the dust cover, noting that medical immortality is not a viable possibility in the near future, man's myth-making capacity would certainly construct the idea from the information in *Prolongevity*.

While genetic engineering and the search for a killer hormone are relatively new, the quest for medical immortality is not. In the Gilgamesh epic, mankind's first great narrative (ca. 3000 B.C.), the hero finds a plant at the bottom of the sea with rejuvenating properties. Unfortunately, a serpent steals the thorny bush from Gilgamesh while he bathes. Like the hero, men of antiquity searched for the secret of eternal life. Mortar and pestle were used to combine plant, animal, and mineral; furnaces were employed in the hope of producing liquid gold, the "elixir of immortality."

Perhaps the thinker who best incorporates the science of antiquity is Roger Bacon, a thirteenth century physicist, chemist, and monk. A precocious forerunner of the scientific age, Bacon championed experimentation as the route to knowledge. Nevertheless in his quest for immortality, he appropriated a variety of earlier approaches. He copied the greatest physician of the ancient world, Galen (A.D. second century), by stressing the importance of diet, exercise, and breathing. Like Arabic thinkers, the Franciscan monk indulged in alchemy, trying to extract liquid gold from lead and other base metals. Following his earlier European counterparts, he found rejuvenating qualities in aloes wood and rosemary, the flesh of snakes, and bones from the heads of stags. He also thought the breath of a virgin could restore one's youth. This last idea had been popular in Christian history, inspired by the story in 1 Kings where moribund King David is kept alive by the warmth of Abishag, a young maiden. In Bacon's day, a long life ended at fifty. The monk believed that through the miracle of science, life expectancy could be raised to 150 years or more.

After Bacon, there were sporadic attempts to engineer immortality. The main thrust of medical thinking, however, was that life could be prolonged, sometimes to great lengths, by eating lightly and avoiding stress. Nevertheless there were adventurers who took more than a hygienic approach toward immortality. In 1492, the famous year of Columbus's voyage, Pope Innocent VIII had the blood of three young men transfused into his veins. The experiment ended his life. In the sixteenth century Paracelsus, arguably the greatest physician of his day, announced he had discovered a cure for death. In spite of his immortality elixir, he died at age forty-eight. In 1766 surgeon and anatomist John Hunter performed the first cryonics experiment. He froze several live carp, and then thawed them slowly. The results were disappointing. Hunter wrote:

> Till this time I had imagined that it might be possible to prolong life to any period by freezing a person in the frigid zone, as I thought all action and waste would cease until the body was thawed. I thought that if a man would give up the last ten years of his life to this kind of alternate oblivion and action, it might be prolonged to a thousand years: and by getting himself thawed every hundred years, he might learn what had happened during his frozen condition.[3]

While Hunter was experimenting with cryonics, a number of other scientists were noting the regenerative aspect of alcohol combined with sunlight. It was thought that flies drowned in wine returned to life when placed outdoors on a sunny day. Could it be possible that humans similarly pickled would revive? Benjamin Franklin, one of our great colonial minds, speculated on the idea. In a letter to a physician carrying out such experiments, Franklin writes that he would love to be

> immersed in a cask of Madeira wine, with a few friends, till that time, to be then recalled to life by solar warmth of my dear country. But since in all probability we live in an age too early and too near infancy of science, to hope to see an art brought in our time to its perfection, I must for the present content myself with the treat, which you are so kind to promise me, of the resurrection of a fowl or a turkey cock.[4]

Perhaps the most famous experiment on longevity was revealed on June 1, 1889. Before the prestigious *Société de Biologie* in Paris, Charles Édouard Brown-Séquard, one of the leading physiologists of the world, told how he injected himself with testicular extracts of a dog and guinea pigs two weeks earlier. The transformation, he told his dumbstruck audience, was remarkable. Although Brown-Séquard was seventy-two, he felt thirty years younger. His muscle tone had improved dramatically and his sexual potency had been restored. He had even married a woman much younger than himself. Although his professional career was ruined after his announcement, Brown-Séquard enjoyed popular success. He created a rejuvenation machine for the benefit of Frenchmen and expounded his theory of longevity to all who would listen. Five years after his announcement, his immortalist hopes ended. His young wife left him, and he died shortly thereafter of a stroke. Brown-Séquard's work triggered similar experiments in the twentieth century and paved the way for future endocrinological research.

Scientific Problems

As we can see from the above examples, there is little similarity between the longevity research conducted in the past and the work Rosenfeld describes today. What scientists of the past and present share is the belief in an imminent breakthrough. Science is on the verge of solving the mysteries of aging and death. Although men like Bacon and Brown-Séquard were mistaken, what about researchers today? Is there a possibility of extending man's lifespan for a few more years, if not indefinitely? Although the verdict is still out, most researchers think not. Expressing the concensus, award winning author and physician Lewis Thomas once stated:

> If we are not struck down, prematurely, by one or another of today's diseases, we live a certain time and then we die, and I doubt that medicine will ever gain the capacity to do anything much to modify this. I can see no reason for trying, and no hope of success anyway. At a certain age, it is in our nature to wear out, to come unhinged and die, and that is that.[5]

Thomas made his comment in 1974 before a meeting of the American College of Surgeons. Nine years later Dr. Eugene Garfield, who edits a magazine devoted to the medical computer research system in this country (*Med-Line*) and who is perhaps the foremost expert on current medical trends, said much the same. "As far as physical immortality is concerned," writes Garfield, "we have not altered the life-to-death scenario in any significant way, so men and women continue to strive for immortality through their children, their creativity, their religion."[6] Certainly Thomas and Garfield's statements carry the weight of history. Throughout the ages, man's maximum lifespan has remained constant—110 years. In America at this time we have been able to increase the average life expectancy to seventy-three years, but our scientific know-how is unable to break the 110-year barrier. There were reports, several years ago, that a few remote societies routinely reached ages well beyond the actuarial ceiling. The diet and work habits of these Russian and Ecuadorian peasants, living in mountainous valleys, were studied assiduously. We were told that a simple diet and a stress free existence were ways to live past 130. Recent studies have shown, however, that those reports of longevity were exaggerations. Few of the peasants are older than a century.[7] Man's maximum lifespan may be more than the biblical three score and ten, but it is still fixed.

The problem with the research of Hayflick and Denckla is that, at present, it is still hypothetical. Concrete evidence is lacking. Dr. Bernard Strehler, a microbiologist at the University of Southern California—and a believer in man's eventual triumph over death—admits nevertheless that the cellular clock of aging has not been proved. He writes:

> At this point in time, eighty per cent through the twentieth century, we still are unable to predict with any degree of certainty the extent to which the aging process will be retarded or arrested for future generations of humans. The reason is quite simple: we lack essential basic information on the origins and mechanisms of age-related cell dysfunctions that gradually lead to a logarithmically increasing disposition to disease and death.[8]

In other words, although scientists can pinpoint the signs of age in a cell, they still cannot tell what triggers aging. Strehler adds that cell research is often contradictory and irrelevant. More money must be thrown into research if we are to understand the cellular clock of aging, if indeed there is one. The problem with Denckla's research is that his death hormone is yet to be discovered. Most scientists doubt that a single hormone is the culprit, although the endocrine system may play a part in the aging process. DECO is, and probably will remain, a hypothetical acronym.

Life has been prolonged by reducing body temperature or restricting diet, but these findings apply to simpler organisms. An amoeba, and even a rat, is far different from a man. The problem is transferring the results to a human scale. There are no parabiotic experiments on humans of which I am aware. Research, too, on modern immortality elixirs like procaine hydrocholoride has been disappointing.[9] Some have been found to relieve attendant problems of aging, like arthritis, but none increases longevity.

From our brief survey, we can see that the idea of medical immortality is premature to say the least, and that many of the books and articles written today are deceptive. They raise hopes that simply cannot be met given our present state of knowledge. Most researchers note that we are fledglings in the aging field. The National Institute on Aging was only established recently, in 1976, and most gerontologists (age researchers) believe there is much catching up to do. Although we might wish immortality were around the corner, at this stage in human history, it is not, nor will it be in the foreseeable future.

Practical Problems

Like the other myths we have examined, belief in Medical Immortality creates problems for the patient and his family. The case of Earl and Kate is typical. Earl had worked as a chemist at a major pharmaceutical firm before he took an early retirement at age forty-five to help run the family business. He had enough experience with science to believe a cure for every disease would be forthcoming. His wife, who had been a pharmacist for several years before they married, also believed science would eliminate obstacles to increased lifespan. Acting on their beliefs, they lived in a secluded country area, grew much of their own food, and eschewed packaged goods with preservatives. They were doing all they could to make it to the golden age.

The Myth of Medical Immortality

When Kate entered the hospital for cancer, she was confident that it could be cured. She experienced great periods of anger, however, when she realized she would not recover. Certainly anger is not uncommon among dying patients. I felt, however, that the intensity of hers was. Before I met her, Kate's husband told me how she dug her fingernails into the doctor's hand one day when he examined her. On another occasion she threw a glass of water at a nurse. Kate was normally a placid individual. From what I could piece together from both parties, it seemed Kate was operating out of a myth mentality. Because she believed science could solve the problem of dying, she became extremely angry at the medical staff for not measuring up to standards.

That health professionals have failed one is a common reaction among the terminally ill. But the myth strengthens this notion. If you are told there is no hope when science is on the verge of solving the mystery of death, then you are in the wrong hospital. Many patients and their families often go through a crazy-quilt time when they call a variety of hospitals, looking for third and fourth opinions. Kate didn't do this. In the back of her mind, she knew she was getting the best possible care.

Kate's wrath was not only directed at the medical staff. She also got angry at fate. This, too, is a common reaction. The terminally ill patient lashes out at life for being cruel and capricious. *Why,* the question is asked, *must I be the one to die?* The myth heightens this emotion. If the immortality breakthrough is imminent, then one realizes the terrible irony of being born a few years, perhaps a few months, too early. Fate, then, seems especially cruel. Earl told me Kate became furious after friends visited, because she believed they would inherit what she would be denied. She would not be one of the scientifically "chosen ones." Perhaps one of the few comforts the terminally ill patient derives is the thought that others must also die. One may get angry because he or she is dying sooner than loved ones or well before the average life expectancy. Nevertheless there is a bit of hope in the fact that everyone must, as Hamlet notes, "shuffle off this mortal coil." Even this sliver of sunlight disappears, however, if the patient believes that in the near future humanity may not die. Death for him becomes more terrible than ever.

Finally Kate got angry at herself. Like Mind over Death, the myth before us also makes the individual responsible for his ultimate future. If the answer to old age and death is around the corner, then one must do everything possible to maintain his health. Indeed keeping fit becomes the quintessential task of the believer. The self-blame factor skyrockets, however, if he gets sick. *Why wasn't I more careful about the way I lived?* he asks himself. *Why didn't I sacrifice in the past for the sake of my future?* Near the end of her life, Kate condemned herself for, among other things, eating candy and drinking cola as a child. She said, in all seriousness, that her evil ways had finally caught up with her at age forty-two. Let me add that in Kate's case there was a crossover in myths. Kate also believed in Mind over Death. Besides blaming herself for what she ate and drank, she also condemned herself for not thinking positive thoughts. Indeed, it seems that often the myth of Mind over Death contributes to the problems engendered by the myth of Medical Immortality.

The problem for Earl was that he, too, blamed Kate for getting sick. Although he never expressed it to her verbally, Earl wondered why Kate had not tried harder to maintain her health, given the imminence of the scientific breakthrough. He told me how she had foolishly given up vitamins several years earlier. And she hadn't thrown herself into jogging the way she once did. Thus belief in the myth caused Earl to blame Kate more than he normally would have, I believe.

Finally Kate experienced fear. Because of her belief in the myth, she was unprepared to face what she had to face. She had no spiritual response on which to draw. It was near the end of her life that she turned to a clergyman, an action neither she nor Earl would have taken in better times.

Why We Believe

The myth of Medical Immortality attracts, obviously, because it offers an answer to what man fears most. Science, as writers like Rosenfeld suggest, can free man from the fear of death by making immortality an empirical fact. Like the Near Death Experience, the myth before us also lends itself to a culture that believes it is historically special. If there is a rejuvenating elixir, it will be discovered in our golden age. There are also two other reasons, unique to the myth itself, that explain its popularity.

First, it fits a culture that has a special fear of growing old. Today we are terrified by the prospect of aging. Throughout history, man has feared the attendant physical problems of longevity. In one of the earliest Greek myths, the goddess of the dawn, Eos, falls in love with Tithonus, a mortal. Eos asks Zeus to bestow immortality on her lover; the chief god of the Greek pantheon obliges. Because Eos fails to asks for eternal youth, however, Tithonus spends eternity in a decrepit state. Through this myth, the Greeks expressed their fear of growing old. The faltering gait, the inability to feed or clothe oneself have been especially frightening to a society whose average lifespan was little more than two decades. In our time, we are not simply frightened by the prospect of invalidism. Because we are obsessed with beauty and dexterity, we panic at the first signs of physiological change. Old age for us begins when the first facial wrinkle appears, or when we sprint a second or two slower than we did the previous year. In Oscar Wilde's chilling novel, *The Picture of Dorian Gray*, Sir Henry Wotton states:

> The pulse of joy that beats in us at twenty, becomes sluggish. Our limbs, our senses rot. We degenerate into hideous puppets, haunted by the passions of which we were too much afraid, and the exquisite temptations that we had not the courage to yield to. Youth! Youth! There is absolutely nothing in the world but youth![10]

This incredible statement may have shocked Wilde's Victorian contemporaries, but it seems run-of-the-mill in our era. Indeed the spirit of Sir Henry lives on in countless commentators who reinforce our understanding of old age whenever they tell us how a model or athlete is "over the hill" before the onset of middle age.

Recently I had an experience that made me aware of our attitude toward aging. I had lunch with a seminarian in his early twenties who mistook me for being a few years older. He said nothing when I mentioned I was thirty-six. Near the end of our meal he asked me, as one might ask a Martian, if life was good at my age. Having spent time with octogenarians who assured me that my prime decades were yet to come, I told my friend that the thirties were much better than the twenties, and that I looked forward to the future. "It's hard to believe," responded the minister-to-be.

Cultural historian Christopher Lasch notes that "men and women begin to fear growing old before they even arrive at middle age.... Americans experience the fortieth birthday as the beginning of the end."[11] Writing in 1978 Lasch's statement is accurate but dated. Today age thirty signals for many the start of the steady decline toward decrepitude and death. Thus the myth of Medical Immortality appeals to a generation that has greatly expanded the definition of old age.

Perhaps, too, the myth attracts because it justifies our obsession with physical fitness. Our love affair with athletics is given a rational base. In his classic study on play and culture, J. Huizinga found that the play element was vanishing from sports in the twentieth century. While certain areas of society have become more playful, Huizinga noted a "fatal shift in overseriousness" in organized sports on a professional level.[12] The Dutch author wrote in the fifties.

Since that time we have seen how this life-and-death attitude has percolated down to the amateur level. Today people pursue athletic goals with the zeal of crusaders hunting for the Holy Grail. Recently Charles Prebish, a professor at Penn State, noted that sports have "replaced traditional religion as a means of reaching ultimate reality."[13] The good professor's remark was not appreciated by his employer, one of the collegiate football capitals of the country. Nevertheless, for me, the truth of his statement is confirmed whenever I see the intensity of the jogging or racquetball enthusiast. Sport is taken seriously because it has become a religion for many. Unable to believe in religions or philosophies that help us transcend self, we construct faiths that worship self. The myth gives this new religion credibility for, indeed, it makes sense to jog our lives away if this practice helps us secure eternal life. If immortality is around the corner, then it seems reasonable to be obsessed with our health.

I am not trying to downplay the importance of exercise to physical and mental health. However, as a Christian I am saying that athletics are a part of life and not, as many Americans believe, life itself.

Once again we examine Christian Everyman and see how different he is from his modern secular counterpart. Everyman understood that it was part of God's plan that he die. He could deal with the attendant problems of old age, because he believed there was divine purpose in infirmity: It weaned him from the world. Everyman's attitude was expressed by a ninety-five-year-old parishioner. When asked how he was doing he responded, "Well enough, but in my condition, I won't be holding on to the couch when God's call comes."

There was also meaning in old age for Everyman, because he believed it conferred wisdom, a quality youth often lacked. The elderly understood the nature of God and life far better than those who were still "wet behind the ears."

Then, too, Everyman valued old age because it meant the individual was that much closer to heaven. Aging was viewed as a progression toward Jesus Christ rather than a regression from a youthful ideal. Because he believed a better world awaited him, it made little sense to prolong his life beyond his three score and ten. Thus Everyman was not particularly health conscious, nor did he spend his days seeking an immortality elixir. In fact, during times of persecution and pestilence, he often prayed that his life would be shortened. Essentially Everyman accepted the provisional nature of this life, and oriented himself toward the next.

Biblical Considerations

Man-made immortality is a nonissue in the Bible. After Adam's attempt to secure eternal life, biblical characters don't bother. There is an incident in the New Testament that, at first glance, might be construed as an attempt to engineer immortality. St. Paul dealt with heretics in the church at Thessalonica who believed the second coming had already taken place and that they were immortal. Their beliefs were conditioned by misguided theology rather than scientific principle. Indeed science of the day—what there was of it—is generally disregarded in the Bible, unlike the religious writings of the Greeks and Egyptians. The practice of medicine, for example, was considered a despised profession in Jesus' country and the Bible usually denigrates astrology, the highest form of science in the ancient world. The notable exception is Matthew's birth narrative, where the magi are guided to Jesus' birthplace by the stars. Generally, however, whether it is medicine or astrology, man's knowledge amounts to little, according to the biblical authors. Especially in the Wisdom literature of the Old Testament, we are told that humans are incapable of understanding the mysteries of the universe let alone solving them. This idea is vividly presented in the book of Job. Man's intellectual limitations are highlighted by a series of confidence-shaking questions God puts to the title character:

> Have you entered the springs of the sea?
> Or have you walked in search of the depths?
> Have the gates of death been revealed to you?
> Or have you seen the doors of the shadow of death?
> Have you comprehended the breadth of the earth?
> Tell Me, if you know all this.

Where is the way to the dwelling of light?
And darkness, where is its place,
that you may take it to its territory,
that you may know its paths to its home?
Do you know it, because you were born then,
or because the number of your days is great? (38:16–21)

As Job is made to understand, man's knowledge is of little account. His task is simply to bend the knee before the great mysteries which God alone understands.

Essentially the idea of man-made immortality is a nonissue because biblical writers could not conceive the value of eternal life without God. The purpose of existence was to commune fully with the Creator of the universe and his Son, Jesus. Earthly life was merely a prelude to lasting fellowship in heaven. Comparing his body to a tent, St. Paul notes, "For we who are in this tent groan, being burdened, not because we want to be unclothed, but further clothed, that mortality may be swallowed up by life" (2 Cor. 5:4). A limitless extension of life would probably be meaningless to someone like the great apostle, who anticipated complete fellowship with Christ only after death.

When we examine God's word, we also realize the biblical writers were not interested in longevity *per se*. It is true the elderly are valued for their wisdom, and great age is often one's reward for serving God. Nevertheless we receive no impression that number of years and meaningful existence are correlated. At least in terms of salvation history, Moses' life was far more meaningful than Methuselah's, although it was much shorter. Indeed Jesus led a perfect life, yet he died long before reaching the ages of major Old Testament figures.

It is interesting to note that the New Testament pays

no attention whatsoever to the length of one's life. Of the four Evangelists, only Luke reveals Jesus' age at two points. The Son of God taught the elders in the Temple at twelve, and then, at thirty, he began his public ministry. The third Evangelist fails to tell us when Jesus died. Although scholars assume he was crucified in his early thirties, there is no explicit reference in the biblical account. Similarly we do not know the lifespans of Jesus' disciples, Paul, or Paul's coworkers. The biblical silence in this area emphasizes the idea that salvation is found in the quality of one's relationship to God rather than the quantity of years.

Although the biblical writers never broach the myth of Medical Immortality, we can see how this idea runs against the biblical grain. The Bible insists that one must decide for God in the present. The day of judgment is at hand. From a biblical perspective, the positive aspect of death is that it serves as the impetus for decision. If one is to have eternal life in the present and future, he must choose God before death robs him of his choice-making capacity. I believe the biblical writers would have understood the danger of an immortality elixir. Given such a potion, the individual would have all the time in the world not to decide for God. He would procrastinate eternal life away.

I do not believe maintaining a biblical stance means opposition to scientific progress as some suggest. I pray that our knowledge will solve the attendant problems of aging. Arthritis and senility are scourges which we hope will be eradicated one day. As a Christian, however, I do not believe man-made immortality is the great panacea. It would not solve man's fear of death. The Grim Reaper would be more frightening, because he would become the exception rather than the rule. If people died from accidents alone, man's fear of death would permeate every corner of his life. Viewing immortality as a never-ending obstacle course, he would reduce meaningful existence to a grim game of self-preservation. Belief in God's promise of eternal life, on the other hand, helps us relativize death, making it possible to risk, to live meaningfully without the fear that one misstep will be our last.

Finally, I do not believe the world would be a better place if the myth of Medical Immortality became a reality. In a postscript to his play *Back to Methuselah*, the English writer George Bernard Shaw wrote:

> On all lands as I write the cry is that our statesmen are too old, and that Leagues of Youth must be formed everywhere to save civilization from them. But despairing ancient pensioners tell me that the young are worse than the old; and the truth seems to be that our statesmen are not old enough for their jobs. Life is too short for the experience and development needed to change romantic schoolboys and golfing sportsmen, or even prematurely forced Quakers, into wise senators....In the case of man, the operation has overshot its mark: men do not live long enough: they are, for all the purposes of high civilization, mere children when they die.[14]

Shaw's understanding of the perfectibility of man is as old as Socrates himself. History teaches, however, that longevity often increases the individual's orientation toward selfishness and evil. With age, tyrants usually become worse, not better. If change comes, it is because of an individual's acceptance of Jesus Christ rather than some innate ability that causes him to grow morally after a period of time. Man's three score and ten, then, serves a positive purpose in ridding the world of Stalins before they can do even more damage.

The myth of Medical Immortality offers no answer to the problems of living or dying. Salvation for man is found in the gospel, not the test tube.

CHAPTER
8

Our Resurrection Hope

In order to free people from the fear of death, we must proclaim the power of the resurrection. The Grim Reaper will not be tamed by cosmeticizing his ugliness, as the myths we have explored try to do. The popularity of death's disguises, however, is not merely evidence of the power of secularism. In a deeper sense it points to the church's failure to proclaim the centrality of the resurrection. There has been little opposition to myths from ecclesiastical sources. In recent history, the theological center of Christianity has been moved to the periphery, often unwittingly, by liberal and conservative factions. From my perspective as a parish minister, the shift has been disastrous. The parishioner is no longer sure what the church believes about his ultimate destiny. Often he is terrified of hospitalization because he no longer thinks divine love can transcend his death.

Sociologist Peter Berger once wrote: "The power of religion depends, in the last resort, upon the credibility of the banners it puts in the hands of men as they stand before death, or more accurately, as they walk, inevitably, toward it."[1] By their word and example, Christian leaders have often given their flock paper flags, which are easily tattered by the whirlwind of terminal illness.

The Bible teaches that eternal life begins in the present and continues after death. There is a present and future aspect to God's great promise. American Christendom stresses the present aspect of continuum. We are told that God's love may extend beyond death, but his concern and ours should be with this life. Paul's words, "If in this life only we have hope in Christ, we are of all men the most pitiable" (1 Cor. 15:19), are viewed as heresy by our here-now brand of Christian. Certainly we must be concerned with faith in the present, especially given the precarious state of our world. Surrounded by the nuclear means to atomize the globe, we must act as courageously as Jesus and the prophets. Doing so, however, does not invalidate the need to stress the reality of eternal communion with the one who calls us some day to rest from our earthly labors.

I have found that both liberal and conservative camps in American Christendom have given the Bible a worldly flavor that subtly distorts God's word. They have done their collective parts to make the idea of eternal life less than a living reality for people in the pew. Before we can hope to correct the imbalance between the present and future orientations, we must first understand the nature of the problem.

Although I generalize in writing about liberalism and conservatism, I am following theological precedent. Recently, for example, Harvey Cox, the eminent theologian from Harvard, used the same categories to carry out his argument. Although the expert may quibble about the theological makeup of a liberal or a conservative, most lay people define themselves as one or the other. In other words, they understand what constitutes a theological liberal or conservative. I meet few moderates! Thus we shall proceed with these general labels.

Liberalism

The most recent brand of theological liberalism got its start during the civil rights movement which blossomed in the midsixties. In the struggle for racial equality, many Christians could no longer ignore biblical implications. If God freed the Israelites from slavery, would he not also sanction a new exodus toward freedom and dignity for a significant segment of the American population? When I was a teen-ager, my pastor was one of the first to march in Selma, Alabama for equal rights. I remember the ridicule he received from parishioners who failed to see the social implications of the gospel. Selma was followed by Saigon. Many Christians took to the streets to fight for the rights of the oppressed in Southeast Asia.

Theological questions were hurled at the corridors of power with the rapidity of mortar rockets in Vietnam: What did the Bible say about the abuse of power? Could one square militarism with the gospel's mandate to love one's enemy? Had national honor become a god in itself? One of the main branches to spread from the trunk of Vietnam was greater concern with the poor and oppressed in Third World countries. Influenced by the thinking of political and liberation theologians, liberals could talk about a "preferential option for the poor" in the Bible. By this they meant that the gospel was primarily for the have-nots and could only be interpreted correctly by them.

I believe American liberalism pointed a prophetic finger at many of our national sins. We have often abused minorities, opted for military might, neglected the poor. Unfortunately theological liberals have set at odds social action and the resurrection hope.

In the sixties the thinking of political theologians from Germany, specifically Wolfhard Pannenburg and Jurgen Moltmann, stressed the importance of viewing social issues through the lens of the kingdom of heaven. They thought that the hope of heaven could spur people into working for its fulfillment in this world. They were neither naive nor heretical enough to think that man alone could usher in paradise. They correctly understood, rather, that the hope of heaven only becomes a reality to modern man when he works to see it instituted in the present. Thus, for example, we can only catch a glimmer of God's future love when we try to institute love in the here and now by changing social structures that mitigate Christ's ethic. The work of Jesus during his public ministry becomes the Christian's guide.

Unfortunately other theologians, following in the footsteps of the German thinkers, nevertheless dissociated the resurrection of the dead from social amelioration. Political theologians from America and Latin America have noted often that the individual's hope of heaven allows him to dismiss the suffering of others. It was thought that focusing on future rewards prevents one from constructing a just society for others. Liberal theologians have also told us that the heart of biblical salvation was used by the rich and powerful to trick the poor and downtrodden. Tyrannical regimes promoted heaven because it served as an opiate for the hungry masses. The hope of Elysian Fields kept the poor from demanding their fair share on earth. Liberal theologians assumed that because (in their opinion) the biblical promise of eternal life had been misused by ruling powers, the concept itself has little value. Thus, for example, in his seminal work, *Black Theology and Black Power*, theologian James Cone dismissed the heaven-oriented spirituals of black slaves as tools of plantation owners to keep their help in check. Cone concluded: "The idea of heaven is irrelevant for Black Theology. The Christian cannot waste time contemplating the next world (if there is a next)."[2] Cone's type of thinking has been prevalent in liberal seminaries since the late sixties.

Can one carry out the social mandates of the gospel while affirming one's personal resurrection hope? I think so. In my own ecclesiastical background, John Calvin, the great sixteenth century Reformer, believed in eternal life, yet was equally concerned with the sewage problem in his hometown of Geneva, Switzerland. The great social reformers of the late nineteenth and early twentieth centuries, Christians like Washington Gladden and Walter Rauschenbusch, believed one's paramount concern should be to feed the hungry and clothe the naked. Nevertheless they expressed their hope in a future life. Today we see the same attitude among people like Mother Theresa of Calcutta. When we look at the Old Testament, we realize the prophets who railed against the evils of their day also expected the Great Day of the Lord. And Jesus, whose life was a model of service, nevertheless looked forward to a future time when he would banquet with his followers once again.

To set the social demands of the gospel against the hope of eternal life is unbiblical. As a parish minister I have seen the negative effects of such thinking in the parish. It may be harmless to link resurrection with social apathy in the rarified atmosphere of seminary, but let loose in a local congregation, this idea is poisonous. I have known ministers, trained in liberal institutions, who make careers out of hectoring congregations for their unconcern with the poor. Ironically, many of these churches commit a sizeable percentage of their budgets to benevolences. Alongside his social action agenda, the minister often downplays or dismisses the needs of his parishioner. Because there are starving children in the world, the person in the pew is told he is selfish to think about his ultimate future. Besides, the resurrection is simply a rich man's ploy against the poor man. Too often parishioners enter hospitals robbed of the hope that is biblically theirs. Recently a neighboring minister told his congregation, on Easter Sunday, that the central message of the resurrection was to rouse the disciples from apathy. He said nothing about the significance of Christ's victory over death.

I believe the reason many liberals downplay the resurrection hope is that they have bought the critical spirit of unbelief which pervades our society. Reality is what can be explained naturally, scientifically. Many have drunk deeply from the well of theologians like Rudolf Bultmann, who once noted that anyone who turns on an electric light cannot believe in the three-tiered universe of the Bible. According to Bultmann and others, if the resurrection has significance, it is metaphorical in nature. Whether actually Jesus was raised from the dead is inconsequential. What matters is that the believer believes in the resurrection whether or not the event occurred. In other words, faith is not grounded in historical reality, but in illusion.

Dismissing the resurrection is fashionable in today's world. Since the midsixties it is chic to slaughter sacred cows wherever they are found in America. Tradition is unimportant. Thus traditional understanding of the faith is, *ipso facto,* suspect. By questioning the reality or importance of the resurrection, the liberal Christian fits in with intellectuals who might have little to do with him otherwise.

By divorcing social action from eternal life, the liberal wing of Christianity has lost its credibility. Careful readers of the Bible, whether or not they are believers, realize that salvation is more than a blueprint for social change. Certainly the strength of American liberalism is that it has often addressed with prophetic candor the great issues of the day, particularly poverty. Its weakness, however, is that it fails to realize the gospel gives hope to the dying as well as to the impoverished, to the individual as well as to the group.

The Bible gives no indication that one is being selfish in thinking about his ultimate destiny or the destiny of loved ones. On the contrary, the number of resurrection appearances in the Gospels indicates the importance of Good News for the individual believer. In the gospel of John, the post-Easter Christ speaks first to one of his followers, Mary Magdalene. In the earliest account of the resurrection—Paul's words in 1 Corinthians 15—we are told that Jesus first appeared to an individual, Peter. Certainly the resurrection hope is by nature hope for the individual, since dying is an event one undergoes alone. Although people can help us, no one can die for us.

I do not mean to criticize all liberal churchmen. What I am saying, however, is that there is a pervasive attitude in American Christendom, fostered by ecclesiastical liberals, that the resurrection is unimportant. What they have given the individual in the pew is a "here only" brand of faith.

Conservatism

Ecclesiastical conservatives also downplay future life with Christ, although in subtler ways. I first became aware of the problem through friends who shared why they could not accept the Christian message. Jesus had to be a memory rather than a living presence, because they did not see the gospel enacted in the church. Their particular stumbling block was the most visible representation of theological conservatism, the television preachers. They believed the displays of wealth and power over the airwaves on Sunday morning clashed with what they read about the itinerant preacher from Nazareth. Paul was correct in noting a laborer was worthy of his keep; my friends felt, however, that Christendom's leaders had overstepped the acceptable moral limit by miles. They said they could no longer tell the difference between the preacher on TV and an entrepreneur.

They may have overstated their case, yet I think their criticism is valid. The concern with money, and the crass way trinkets are hawked, foster the notion that Christianity is primarily concerned with the things of this world. Television spokesmen may talk about eternal life, but spiritual reality is undermined by the materialistic attitude displayed on the screen.

Here-now Christianity also extends to the book publishing market. From the preponderance of books, we know that faith will help one solve the small, mundane problems of everyday life. We learn far more about how Christ will help us lose weight than we do about how he will save us from the fear of death. What conservatives have done is trivialize the Christian message. Certainly faith should help us deal with the problems of human existence. If we do not experience Christ's transforming presence today, there is little sense in trusting him in the future. Unfortunately the publishing milieu often gives the impression that ultimate salvation means losing weight, gaining self-confidence, saving the marriage, regaining health, whatever. Christianity is reduced to a here-now hope alone. To compound the problem, some of these books picture earthly salvation in materialist terms: If you have faith, God will shower you with all sorts of earthly goodies. Indeed some books reduce the gospel to a business proposition: If you give a certain amount of money, God will double, triple, or quadruple your investment.

The popularity of television preachers and religious books indicates the here-now nature of conservatism in America. Although eternal life is proclaimed from pulpits, I get the impression that to many preachers life after death is not as important—or as exciting—as the present miracle, whether it is losing a hundred pounds, kicking the alcohol habit, or winning the lottery. We hear little about life "beyond this vale." Again I am not criticizing individual churchmen. What I am saying is that there is an attitude fostered by ecclesiastical conservatism that emphasizes present benefits almost to the exclusion of future hope.

What We Must Do

In order to make eternal communion with Christ a living hope, we must do more than proclaim the resurrection of Jesus Christ on Easter morning. This great event should be incorporated into the preaching cycle throughout the year. Besides preaching, we must also teach. I find many Christians are confused about the basics. They believe, for example, that their physical bodies will be resurrected, an idea that doesn't thrill the elderly I encounter. Or Christians believe certain cultural images of what heaven is like—stock ideas that inspire little confidence. I have a friend who once noted that if heaven meant sitting on a cloud, strumming a harp, then, anyone with two wits to rub together would prefer hell.

What do we preach? What do we teach? Essentially the New Testament proclaims a general resurrection of the dead when God brings down the curtain of history. All who have lived will be brought back to life—some to eternal fellowship with Christ, others to damnation. In that glorious day, the individual will be given a spiritual body, Paul tells us. While denying a materialist view of the afterlife, the great apostle maintains that we need some sort of body to express who we are. The Bible states that the general resurrection will take place at the end of history. But it also indicates that we are with Christ the moment we die. In Luke's crucifixion account, Jesus tells the penitent thief that he will join him in paradise that same day (see 23:43). In the parable of the rich man and Lazarus (Luke 16:19–31), our Lord talks about "Abraham's bosom" where Lazarus departs the moment he dies. *Paradise* and *Abraham's bosom* were contemporary Jewish terms for the lodging of the righteous prior to resurrection. In my pastoral work with the dying, I stress the idea of communion with Christ the moment one dies. In some mysterious way, beyond our comprehension, we are united with One who knows and loves us better than we do ourselves.

While it is important to stress the basics, it is equally important to fill out the biblical hints of what our resurrected state will be like. Commentators have noted that our task is not to explore heaven, as it were, since the writers do not. If a full description of what awaited us were important, this information would have been included, it is argued. There is some truth to this line of reasoning. When we examine literature contemporaneous with the New Testament writings, we realize that much of it stressed the material rewards of heaven. Often the afterlife was pictured as a carbon copy of the present, replete with fig trees, cattle, and wonderful rivers. Much of the writing was akin to the book of Revelation.

In the New Testament as a whole, however, there is a deemphasis on the details of heaven. I believe the writers understood that enumerating specifics would destroy the idea of afterlife for the believer. Poets understand better than many that whenever an idea is concretized, it loses its power. The biblical writers, in this sense, were poets. What the New Testament points to is a reality far greater than words can describe.

Does the Bible's relative silence about heavenly specifics mean the believer should ignore the issue? I think not. I believe there are enough clues about the afterlife, sprinkled throughout the biblical narrative, to spark our imagination and invite our projection. The information we possess calls for personal expansion. One of the most important examples is Paul's analogy between humans and seeds in 1 Corinthians 15:35–45. Although Paul is writing specifically about the difference between one's mortal and one's resurrected body, we get the impression that he is also comparing the nature of existence in the present with the future life. Paul implies that there will be a completion, a filling out of our personalities when we assume the image of the "heavenly Man" (v. 48). We wish Paul were more explicit, and yet, I believe, there is meaning in his reticence. We are called to ask ourselves, "How will I grow in Christ?" "What aspects of personality will be magnified after death?" "How will I be perfected, completed?" I think there are moments in our lives when we catch glimpses of the people God intended us to be. We understand, albeit fleetingly, our place in God's grand scheme.

I had a friend who found himself whenever he went hiking in the mountains. He could understand why the biblical writers venerated high places, for he, too, encountered God on mountaintops. I told him that his brief feeling of completeness would be a constant in the future life. I didn't paint pictures of mountains in heaven. Such an image would not have sparked his imagination. Rather I tried to focus on the feeling of wholeness: God had touched him in part during his hikes; someday God would touch him completely. The feeling would be magnified.

I am saying we must personalize the resurrection hope. Our ultimate destiny is not to be angels devoid of personality or cardboard saints, but rather the individuals we were intended by God to be at the beginning of our lives. The glimpses of completeness we experience in this life are one of the best indications we have of what future life will be like.

We must do more than personalize the resurrection hope, however. We must also bring out its relational aspect. One never evolves in a vacuum. We begin to understand God's purpose for our lives in relationship to others. The few references we have to the kingdom of heaven in the Gospels are corporate in nature. God's coming rule is analogous to a banquet or wedding feast. Our Lord says little more—purposely, I believe. We are asked to complete the picture personally. How has fellowship with the communion of saints—be it family, friends, congregation—helped us to realize who we truly are? In the presence of whom are we the individuals God calls us to be? I have often found in my work that a terminally ill patient's hope in the future is to fellowship with those he has loved and lost through death. Once an eighty-five-year-old parishioner, dying of cancer, told me she longed to crawl up on her mother's lap, as she did many years earlier, and be comforted. She was most herself, she believed, in that relationship. I said that in some way, beyond our comprehension, that comforting relationship would be restored.

At this juncture, however, I raise a biblical problem. Although we can speak about the gathering together of the family of God in the kingdom of heaven, can we talk with equal confidence about the reestablishment of personal relationships that have meant most to us? At first glance the answer seems to be no.

In the Gospels there is a scene in which the Sadducees question Jesus about the resurrection by imposing a hypothetical problem. Suppose a woman's husband dies and leaves her without children? According to the law of the Old Testament, it was a brother's obligation to marry his sister-in-law for the purpose of procreation. Further, suppose the husband had six brothers, all of whom married the woman without giving her children? Whose wife would she be in the resurrection? Jesus responds by saying, "For when they rise from the dead, they neither marry nor are given in marriage, but are like the angels in heaven" (Mark 12:25). His words seem to indicate that the relationships we value most will not be restored. Yet I think we must view Christ's words contextually.

Jesus was not offering a description of the afterlife as much as he was refuting the *reductio ad absurdum* question of a hostile party. The Sadducees were not interested in heaven. They did not believe in it, unlike the other major party, the Pharisees. Their question was designed to point up the foolishness of belief in the afterlife. Jesus' answer was a reaction against the intent of their question. He dismisses it by saying that the resurrected life is different from the life we know, and that to believe heaven is a carbon copy of present existence is to misunderstand the power of God. Heaven is far greater, Jesus implies, than the minute elements of earthly existence. His line of argument, in this context, does not rule out similarity between this life and the life to come.

The Last Supper, for example, was instituted by our Lord as an eschatological meal: it tells the disciples what to expect in heaven. The physical accouterments at this sacred meal are unimportant. Whether we will be eating from gold or silver goblets in the future is unimportant. Whether we fellowship in an earthly manner—literally eating and drinking—is also unimportant. What matters is that someday we will be together. In the same manner, I believe the specific nature of our closest relationships is unimportant in the future kingdom. Whether we live together, once again, in a cozy Cape Cod by the sea is unimportant. Whether we share the same kinds of hobbies or interests is unimportant. What matters, what will be preserved and magnified, is the love for one another, devoid of particulars, which has energized us in this life. Someday we will be together with those we have loved most.

If the resurrection hope is to be a living reality, the church must remove its theological blinders and confront the challenge. If it refuses, bogus forms of salvation will continue to flourish. Men and women look to the church for the hope they need to confront that which frightens them most. They should not be told that dying is natural, beautiful, or euphoric. It isn't. They should not be told that science has solved the enigma of death itself. It hasn't. In the grip of terminal illness, the patient sees through the ruses we employ to disguise the nature of death. People must be told, again and again, that they can face the Grim Reaper triumphantly, but only because of the power of Jesus Christ, our resurrected Lord.

Eternal Life and My Present Existence

As my faith has grown through the years, the thought of eternal life not only frees me from the fear of death; it enables me *to live fully in this life*. When I was starting out in my career, I could not forgive myself for bad decisions or mistakes. In viewing my actions through the prism of eternity, however, I am able to view poor choices as less than catastrophic in nature. Focusing on eternal life also makes me better able to risk for others. A couple of years ago, on a tour of the Holy Land, I visited a friend living in the old city of Jerusalem. One is told not to venture into my friend's section of town after sunset. Belief in eternal fellowship helped me to step into the unlit cobblestone street without worrying about the future.

Similarly, a couple of years ago I walked into the hospital room of a tubercular patient without donning a surgical mask. I came closer to him than I normally would, during my prayer, because he was hard of hearing. In retrospect I realized I had forgotten the mask. "Reverend Hygiene" would not have let this *faux pas* occur several years earlier. I realize now that the risk factor no longer concerned me. I do not mean to imply that I am playing Russian roulette with my life, deliberately tempting death. It is rather that increased faith in the afterlife allows me to live the way Christ intended, free from the constraint of a safety-first mentality.

As my faith in eternal life has grown, I am also better able to let go of those I have lost through death. I think the parish ministry is emotionally draining because the congregation becomes part of a minister's family. Through the course of a pastorate, you bury a number of parishioners whom you view as brothers and sisters. I remember the shock I experienced at 5:00 A.M. one Easter Sunday morning when a forty-eight-year-old member of the church died of a massive heart attack. Art had seemed in perfect health. We had taken the youth group roller skating the night before, and he had been the best skater on the floor. Several hours later, I stood beside his wife in a cubicle near the emergency room reserved for the dead and their relatives. I remember thinking that I could no longer manage this gut-wrenching job. Today, however, I realize more fully that the "Arts" in my life are never really lost to me, nor, for that matter, are those to whom I owe great spiritual debts.

While my father fought in Korea and my mother worked full-time as a church secretary, I spent my earliest years in a large Victorian home with three elderly people: Abigail, her sister Kate, and Kate's husband, Leslie. They had taken my mother in as a boarder and maintained a standoffish air until I was born. Abigail, white-haired and statuesque, lost her husband when he was in his late twenties. She had sent him away to a sanatorium in upstate New York, and he never returned. Several years later she watched her daughter die of appendicitis. The girl had celebrated her thirteenth birthday two weeks earlier. Les and Kate went to a variety of specialists because they wanted children. They never had them.

My squalling presence seemed to mend dreams life

had shattered decades earlier. Abbey gave me my first haircut. Les and Kate abandoned their comfortable sofa to sit on Oriental rugs that graced their home and teach me card and marble games. The great French novelist, Marcel Proust, was correct in noting that we remember primarily smells and sounds. I remember the redolence of lavender, the smell of egg custard and apple crisp. Perhaps I first learned what holiness meant, listening to the sound of brass chimes echoing down the hall whenever a visitor approached the door. Abbey, Kate, and Les died in rapid succession before I reached twenty. In other words, they died before I truly realized what they had meant to me. I never had the chance to thank them for their love. This sin of omission bothers me less because I know someday, in God's great future, I will be able to express my gratitude to them.

As my faith in God's great promise has grown, I am better able to live with the mysteries of my life. For the most part, I find that Christ reveals his will in the fullness of history. We may not understand why things happen to us when they do. Nevertheless, weeks, months, or years later we see how an event, even the most painful, worked to God's glory and our salvation. And yet there are aspects of our lives that, I think, we never fully understand. Why did a loved one die? Why did a member of the family experience an unwarranted tragedy? Why have we suffered?

Recently I experienced an event that befalls 50 per cent of the couples who marry—divorce. It is one of the most difficult processes one can undergo. Jesus was not using a figure of speech when he noted that two become one in a marriage. There is a metaphysical bond that exists in the worst of unions, a link created by God. Once it is sundered, the two parties are rarely, if ever, the same. In my case (and the cases of many ministers, I believe), I felt torn between my calling and a woman who believed my vocation diminished her. Why the marriage did not work, why it could not work is one of the great mysteries of my life. I doubt if I will ever resolve the issue on earth. Yet as my faith grows, I am better able to live with the human enigmas reason cannot solve, knowing that someday, in God's kingdom, the answers will be clear.

Finally, increased faith in the afterlife has helped me become a little more relaxed in the area of knowledge. At one time I thought my life would be meaningless if I failed to read most of the great literary masterpieces before I died. I mistakenly believed that what I valued would be lost at death. In other words, although I confessed my belief in the resurrection, I did not see its connection with my spiritual and intellectual growth. Perhaps I had a conception of heaven similar to that of a funeral parlor. My ultimate destiny was to be in a recumbent and mindless state, smiling at Christ for eternity. Now I believe I will take my desire to learn with me and that, in the effulgence of Christ's knowledge, my desire will be satisfied. In the gospel of John, Jesus states: "In My Father's house are many mansions" (14:2). The Greek word for *mansions* may also be translated as "stations along the way" or "temporary dwellings"; I find this meaning appealing. Perhaps we shall progress through stages of growth, as we have in this life. The gospel does not elaborate; neither shall I.

I can live with spiritual and intellectual incompleteness because I know someday, I will be completed. Someday I shall become fully one with myself, with others, and with my gracious savior, even Jesus Christ our risen Lord.

Notes

Introduction

1. Elisabeth Kubler-Ross, *To Live Until We Say Good-bye*, (Englewood Cliffs, N.J.: Prentice-Hall, 1978), 12.

Chapter 1

1. *Life*, Nov. 21, 1969, 42.
2. Ibid., 42.
3. *The Christian Herald*, New York, John E. Caldwell, ed., 1817, Vol. 3, 334.
4. Elisabeth Kubler-Ross, *On Death and Dying*, (New York: Macmillan,1970), 9.

Chapter 2

1. Earl Grollman, *Talking About Death: A Dialogue Between Parent and Child*, (Boston: Beacon Press, 1976), 2-3.
2. Barry Neil and Suzi Lyte Kaufman, *A Land Beyond Tears*, (New York: Doubleday, 1982), 154.
3. Kubler-Ross, *On Death and Dying*, 120.
4. Ibid., 120.
5. David Cole Gordon, *Overcoming the Fear of Death*, (New York: Macmillan, 1970), 106.
6. Kubler-Ross, *Until We Say Good-bye*, 12.
7. Ibid., 29.
8. See articles in *Psychosocial Care of the Dying Patient*, ed. by Charles Garfield (McGraw-Hill, 1978).
9. *Time*, Jan. 1, 1973, 36.

10. *Shanti Nilaya Newsletter,* No. 15, June, 1983.

11. Ibid.

12. Ibid.

13. Alan Harrington, *The Immortalist: An Approach to the Engineering of Man's Divinity,* (New York: Random House, 1969), 208.

14. Ibid., 21–22.

15. Alvin Silverstein, *Conquest of Death,* (New York: Macmillan, 1979).

16. Norman Cousins, *Anatomy of an Illness: As Perceived by the Patient,* (New York: Bantam, 1981), 139.

17. Hans Selye, *Stress of Life,* (New York: McGraw-Hill, 1956).

18. *Omega Fitness Newsletter,* 1979.

19. David Smith and Judith Granbois, "The American Way of Hospice," *The Hastings Center Report,* April, 1982.

20. *Hospice of Ulster County Newsletter,* Spring, 1981.

21. Stephen Levine, *Who Dies?: An Investigation of Conscious Living and Conscious Dying,* (Garden City, N.Y.: Anchor Press/Doubleday, 1982), 135.

Chapter 3

1. W.J.S. Gravesande, *Mathematical Elements of Natural Philosophy,* 1, ix, quoted in Charles C. Gillispie, *Genesis and Geology* (New York: Harper Torchbooks, 1959), 12.

2. William Buckland, *Vindicae Geologicae; Or The Connexion of Geology with Religion Explained* (Oxford, 1820), quoted in Gillispie, *Genesis,* 103.

3. Charles Darwin, *The Descent of Man and Selection in Relation to Sex* (London: Murray, 1871), 528.

4. Basil Willey, *Nineteenth Century Studies* (London: Chatto and Windus, 1950), 252.

5. Arthur Schlesinger, Sr. "A Critical Period in American Religion, 1875–1900," in *Religion in American History: Interpretive Essays,* John M. Mulder and John F. Wilson, ed., (Englewood Cliffs, N.J.: Prentice-Hall, 1978), 306.

6. James McCosh, *Christianity and Positivism* (New York, 1871), 63–64.

7. Shailer Matthews, *The Faith of Modernism,* quoted in *American Christianity: An Historical Interpretation with Representative Documents,* ed. by H. Shelton Smith, Robert T. Handy, and Lefferts A. Loetscher, Vol. 2 (New York: Scribner's, 1963), 238–239.

Notes

8. Ibid., 241.

9. John Fiske, *Edward Livingston Youmans* (New York: D. Appleton & Co., 1894), 266.

10. Richard Hofstadter, *Social Darwinism in American Thought* (Boston: Beacon Press, 1955), 30.

11. Lymann Abbott, *The Theology of an Evolutionist* (Boston: Houghton Mifflin, 1897), 68.

12. John Parsons, *The Credentials of Science, The Warrant of Faith* (New York: Robert Carter & Brothers, 1888).

13. Henry Harbaugh, *Heaven; Or an Earnest and Scriptural Inquiry into the Abode of the Sainted Dead* (Philadelphia, 1853), 3:17.

14. Elizabeth Stuart Phelps, *The Gates Ajar*, ed. by Helen Sootin Smith (Cambridge, 1964), xxi.

15. Elizabeth Stuart Phelps, *The Gates Ajar* (Fields, Osgood, & Co., 1869), 135.

16. James Stevens Curl, *The Victorian Celebration of Death* (Devon: David and Charles [Publishers], Ltd., 1972), 179.

17. Charles L. Wallis, *Stories on Stone* (New York: Oxford Univ. Press, 1954), 182, 119. On funeral statuary see Edmund V. Gillon, Jr., *Victorian Cemetery Art* (New York: Dover Publications, 1972).

18. Excerpted from the poem "What is Death?" in McGuffey's *New Fourth Eclectic Reader* (Cincinnati: Wilson, Hinkle & Co., 1866), 110.

19. Methodist Hymnal, Philadelphia, 1878.

20. Edward A. Filene, "The Phantom of National Distribution," *Printers' Ink*, cxxiv, No. 12 (Sept. 20, 1923), 180.

21. Edward L. Bernays, *Propaganda* (1928), 47–48.

22. Floyd Henry Allport, *Social Psychology* (1924), 325.

23. *Ladies Home Journal*, April, 1920.

24. Otto Ruhle, *Karl Marx—His Life and Work* (New York: New Home Library, 1926), 366.

25. Sigmund Freud, *The Future of an Illusion* (Garden City, N.Y.: Doubleday, 1953), 102.

26. William E. Phipps, "Darwin the Scientific Creationist," *The Christian Century*, Sept. 14–21, 1983, 811.

27. David McLellan, *Karl Marx: His Life and Thought* (New York: Harper and Row, 1973), 42.

28. Sigmund Freud, *Civilization and Its Discontents*, edited by James Strachey (New York: W.W. Norton, 1961), 21.

29. *Chronicle of Higher Education*, January 9, 1978.

30. Jacques Barzun, *Science: The Glorious Entertainment* (New York: Harper and Row, 1964), 14–15.

31. Stanislav Andreski, "Science as Sorcery," *Time*, Sept. 25, 1972, 71.

32. Marcel Chotkowski La Follette, ed., *Creationism, Science, and the Law: The Arkansas Case* (Cambridge: MIT Press, 1984), 36.

33. Christopher Lasch, *The Culture of Narcissism* (New York: W.W. Norton, 1979), 74.

34. Isaac Asimov, "The Threat of Creationism," *New York Times Magazine*, June 14, 1981, 93.

35. Theodore Roszak, *Where the Wasteland Ends* (Garden City, N.Y.: Doubleday, 1972), 33.

Chapter 4

1. George Fitchett, "It's Time to Bury the Stage Theory of Death and Dying," *Oncology Nurse Exchange*, Vol. 2, Issue 3, Fall, 1980.

2. Elisabeth Kubler-Ross, *Questions and Answers on Death and Dying*, (New York: Macmillan, 1974), 25-26.

3. Ibid., 31.

4. Kubler-Ross, *On Death and Dying*, 39.

5. Elisabeth Kubler-Ross, *Living with Death and Dying*, (New York: Macmillan, 1981), 25.

6. Ibid., 35.

7. Ibid., 38.

8. Kubler-Ross, *On Death and Dying*, 112.

9. Ibid., 113.

10. Kubler-Ross, *Questions and Answers*, 34.

11. Kubler-Ross, *Until We Say Good-bye*, 12.

12. *People*, Oct. 29, 1979.

13. Robert Kastenbaum, *Death, Society, and Human Experience*, (St. Louis: C.V. Mosby, 1977), 210. Kastenbaum, director of the Adult Development Center at Arizona State University, is one of the key people doing scientifically valid research in the area of death and dying. Perhaps the leader in this field is Robert Fulton, director of the Center for Death Education and Research at the University of Minnesota.

14. Edwin Shneidman, *Death of Man*, (Baltimore: Penguin, 1974), 6.

15. J.M. Hinton, "The Physical and Mental Distress of Dying," *Quarterly Journal of Medicine*, 1963, 32, 1-21; K.A. Achte and M.L.

Notes

Vauhkonen, "Cancer and the Psyche," *Omega*, 1971, 2, 46-56; M.A. Lieberman, "Psychological Correlates of Impending Death: Some Preliminary Observations," *Journal of Gerontology*, 1965, 20, 181-190.

16. Charles A. Garfield, "Elements of Psychosocial Oncology: Doctor-Patient Relationships in Terminal Illness," in *Psychosocial Care of the Dying Patient*, ed. by Garfield, (McGraw-Hill, 1978), 112.

17. Kastenbaum, *Death, Society, and Human Experience*; Richard A. Kalish, "A Little Myth Is a Dangerous Thing: Research in the Service of Dying," in Garfield, *Psychosocial Care*; Garfield, "Elements of Psychosocial Oncology."

18. Fitchett, "It's Time to Bury the Stage Theory."

19. George Kuykendall, "Care for the Dying: A Kubler-Ross Critique," *Theology Today*, Vol. 38, No. 1, April, 1981, 40.

20. A. Leveton, "Time, Death, and the Ego Chill," *Journal of Existentialism*, 6, (1965), 75.

21. Three of the most famous stage theories are found in: Carl Nighswonger, "Dying as a Learning Encounter," *Journal of Pastoral Care*, 26 (1972); Avery Weisman "Thanatology," in *Comprehensive Textbook of Psychiatry* in Kaplan et. al. eds. (Baltimore: Williams and Wilkins, 1980); E. Mansell Pattison, "The Experience of Dying," in *The Experience of Dying*, ed. by Pattison, (Englewood Cliffs, N.J.: Prentice-Hall, 1977).

22. Robert P. Hudson, "Death, Dying, and the Zealous Phase," *Annals of Internal Medicine*, 88, (1978), 700.

23. Albert Camus, *The Stranger*, (New York: Random House, 1954), 1.

24. T.S. Eliot, "The Dry Savages," in *The Complete Poems and Plays 1909-1950* (New York: Harcourt Brace Jovanovich, 1971).

25. Nathan A. Scott, Jr., "The Modern Imagination of Death," in *The End of Life*, ed. by John D. Roslansky, (Amsterdam: North-Holland Publishing Co. 1973), 72.

26. Richard Sennett, "Twilight of the Tenured Composer," *Harper's*, Dec., 1984, 72.

27. Aldous Huxley, *Brave New World*, (New York: Harper & Row, 1969), 162.

28. Seneca's quote is found in: Martin Hengel, *Crucifixion*, (Philadelphia: Fortress Press, 1977), 30.

29. Sigmund Freud, "Thoughts for the Times on War and Death," *Collected Papers*, Vol. 4 (London: Hogarth, 1915).

30. Avery D. Weisman, *On Dying and Denying: A Psychiatric Study of Terminality*, (New York: Behavioral Publications, 1972), 100.

An Enemy Disguised

Chapter 5

1. Raymond Moody, *Life After Life*, (New York: Bantam, 1975), 30.

2. Ibid., 32.

3. Ibid., 55–56.

4. Ibid., 59.

5. Russell Noyes, Jr., and Roy Kletti, "Depersonalization in the Face of Life Threatening Danger," *Psychiatry*, 39, Feb., 1976, 19.

6. Moody, *Life After Life*, 16.

7. Ian Stevenson, "Research into the Evidence of Man's Survival After Death," *The Journal of Nervous and Mental Disease*, Vol. 165, No. 3 (1977), 161.

8. See Ronald K. Siegel, "Accounting for Afterlife Experiences," *Psychology Today*, (Jan., 1981), 65–75.; Ronald K. Siegel, "The Psychology of Life After Death," *American Psychologist*, 35 (1980), 911–931.; Ronald K. Siegel and Louis Jolyon West, eds., *Hallucinations: Behavior, Experience and Theory* (Wiley Publishing House, 1975).

9. Roland Puccetti, "The Experience of Dying," *The Humanist*, Vol. 39, 4, (July–Aug., 1979), 64.

10. Robert N. Butler, "The Life Review: An Interpretation of Reminiscence in the Aged," *Psychiatry*, 26, (1963), 65–76.; Donald W. Tripp, "Heavenly Visions and the Process of Grief" (unpublished manuscript, 1978).

11. L. Eugene Thomas, Pamela E. Cooper, and Davic Suscovich, "Incidence of Near-Death and Intense Spiritual Experiences in an Intergenerational Sample: An Interpretation," *Omega*, Vol. 13, 1, (1982–83), 35–41.

12. Russell Noyes, Jr., and Roy Kletti, "Depersonalization in the Face of Life Threatening Danger: An Interpretation," *Omega*, Vol. 7, 2, (1976), 112–113. See also J.A. Arlow, "Depersonalization and Derealization" in *Psychoanalysis in General Psychology*, R.M. Lowenstein, L.M. Newman, M. Schur, and A.J. Solnit, eds. (New York: International Univ. Press, 1966).

13. See Karlis Osis and Erlander Haraldson, *At the Hour of Death*, (New York: Avon Books, 1977); Eckhart Wiesenhutter, *Blick Nach Druben: Selbsterfahrung im Sterben*, (Gutersloh, 1974); Johann Christoph Hampe. *Sterben ist Doch Ganz Anders: Erfahrungen mit dem Eigenen Tod*, (Stuttgart, 1975).

14. George Gallup, Jr., *Adventures in Immortality* (New York: Mc-Graw-Hill, 1982), 123.

15. Flannery O'Connor, *The Complete Stories*, (New York: Farrar, Straus and Giroux, 1953), 316.

16. Daniel L. Migliore, "Life Beyond Death," *Theology Today*, Vol. 34, No. 2, (July, 1977), 180.

17. A.J. Boyle, *The Ecologues of Virgil*, (Melbourne: Hawthorne Press, 1976), 57, 59.

18. Tom Wolfe, *In Our Time* (New York: Farrar, Straus and Giroux, 1980), 11.

19. Pierre Teilhard de Chardin, *The Divine Milieu: An Essay on the Interior Life* (New York: Harper and Brothers, 1960), 62.

Chapter 6

1. Georg Groddeck, *The Book of The It: Psychoanalytic Letters to a Friend* (New York: Nervous and Mental Disease Publishing Co. 1928), 93.

2. National Center for Health Statistics, Vol. 33, No. 9 Supp., Dec. 20, 1984, 3, 41.

3. "Cancer Facts and Figures, 1983," (New York: American Cancer Society, 1982), 3.

4. J. Burrows, *A New Practical Essay on Cancer*, (London, 1783).

5. G. von Schmitt, *On the Curability of Cancer*, (Paris, 1871).

6. Ephram Cutter, "Diet on Cancer," *Albany Medical Annals*, July–August, 1887.

7. Walter Hayle Walshe, *Nature and Treatment of Cancer* (London: 1846).

8. Richard Guy, *An Essay on Scirrhous Tumours and Cancers*, (London: 1759).

9. Robert Burton, *The Anatomy of Melancholy*, Vol. 1, (New York: W.J. Widdleton, Publisher, 1865), 332–333.

10. Jimmie C. Holland, "Psychological Aspects of Cancer," in *Cancer Medicine*, ed. by James F. Holland and Emil Frei III, (Philadelphia: Lea and Febiger, 1982), 1199.

11. Edward J. Beatti, Jr., *Toward the Conquest of Cancer*, (New York: Crown Publishers, 1980), 180.

12. C.L. Bacon, R. Renneker, and M. Cutler: "A Psychosomatic Survey of Cancer of the Breast," *Psychosomatic Medicine*, 14:453, (1952); G. M. Perrin, I. R. Pierce, Psychosomatic Aspects of Cancer,"*Psychosomatic Medicine*, 21:397, (1959); M. Reznikoff, "Psychological

Factors in Breast Cancer: A Preliminary Study of the Same Personality Trends in Patients with Cancer of the Breast"; J.C. Holland, R. Mastrovito, "Psychological Adaptation to Breast Cancer," *Cancer,* 46, 1045–1052, (1980).

13. Mary G. Marcus, "The Shaky Link Between Cancer and Character," *Psychology Today,* June, 1976, 60.

14. Bernard Fox, "Premorbid Psychological Factors as Related to Cancer Incidence," *Journal of Behavioral Medicine,* 1:45 (1978); see also F.G. Surawicz, D.R. Brightwell, W.D. Weitzel, E. Othmer, "Cancer, Emotions, and Mental Illness: The Present State of Understanding," *American Journal of Psychiatry,* 133:11, Nov., 1976.

15. See also A. Peck, "Emotional Reactions to Having Cancer," *American Journal of Roentgenology,* 114: 591–599, (1972).

16. F. Finn, R. Mulcahy, N. Hickey, "The Psychological Profiles of Coronary & Cancer Patients and of Matched Controls," *Journal of Medical Science,* 143: 176–178, May, 1974.

17. Gregory McQuerter, "Cancer: Clues in the Mind," *Science News,* Jan. 21, 1978, 45.

18. Robert Ringer, *Winning Through Intimidation,* (New York: Funk and Wagnalls, 1974), 234.

19. Susan Sontag, *Illness as Metaphor,* Vintage Book Edition (New York: Random House, 1979), 7.

20. Alexis de Tocqueville, *Democracy in America,* (New York: Knopf, 1951), Vol. 2, 99.

21. Peter Marin, "The New Narcissism," *Harper's,* Oct., 1975.

Chapter 7

1. Albert Rosenfeld, *Prolongevity,* (New York: Knopf, 1976), 166.

2. Ibid., 12–13.

3. John Hunter, *Lectures on the Principles of Surgery,* (Philadelphia, 1841).

4. William Pepper, *The Medical Side of Benjamin Franklin,* (Philadelphia, 1911).

5. Lewis Thomas, "The Future Impact of Science and Technology on Medicine," *American College of Surgeons Bulletin,* June, 1974.

6. Eugene Garfield, "The Dilemma of Prolongevity Research," *Current Contents,* Vol. 26, No. 15, April 11, 1983, 5.

Notes

7. Joseph Freeman, "The Old, Old, Very Old Charlie Smith," *The Gerontologist*, (Dec. 1982).

8. Bernard L. Strehler, "Aging Research: Current and Future," *The Journal of Investigative Dermatology*, Vol. 73, No. 1, (1979), 2.

9. Saul Kent, "The Procaine 'Youth' Drugs," *Geriatrics*, April, 1982.

10. Oscar Wilde, *The Picture of Dorian Gray*, (London: Penguin Books, 1984), 30.

11. Christopher Lasch, *The Culture of Narcissism*, (New York: W.W. Norton, 1978), 210.

12. J. Huizinga, *Homo Ludens: A Study of the Play-Element in Culture*, (Boston: Beacon Press, 1950), 198.

13. *U.S. News and World Report*, August 13, 1984, 23.

14. George Bernard Shaw, "Back to Methuselah," in *Complete Plays with Prefaces*, (New York: Dodd, Mead, 1962), ci., xix.

Chapter 8

1. Peter L. Berger, *The Sacred Canopy: Elements of a Sociological Theory of Religion*, (Garden City, N.Y.: Doubleday Anchor, 1969), 51.

2. James H. Cone, *Black Theology and Black Power*, (New York: Seabury, 1969), 125.